# Library Management

# PRACTICAL GUIDES FOR LIBRARIANS

## About the Series

This innovative series written and edited for librarians by librarians provides authoritative, practical information and guidance on a wide spectrum of library processes and operations.

Books in the series are focused, describing practical and innovative solutions to a problem facing today's librarian and delivering step-by-step guidance for planning, creating, implementing, managing, and evaluating a wide range of services and programs.

The books are aimed at beginning and intermediate librarians needing basic instruction/guidance in a specific subject and at experienced librarians who need to gain knowledge in a new area or guidance in implementing a new program/service.

## About the Series Editor

The **Practical Guides for Librarians** series was conceived by and is edited by M. Sandra Wood, MLS, MBA, AHIP, FMLA, Librarian Emerita, Penn State University Libraries from 2014-2017.

M. Sandra Wood was a librarian at the George T. Harrell Library, the Milton S. Hershey Medical Center, College of Medicine, Pennsylvania State University, Hershey, PA, for over thirty-five years, specializing in reference, educational, and database services. Ms. Wood received an MLS from Indiana University and an MBA from the University of Maryland. She is a fellow of the Medical Library Association and served as a member of MLA's Board of Directors from 1991 to 1995.

Ellyssa Kroski assumed editorial responsibilities for the series beginning in 2017. She is the director of Information Technology at the New York Law Institute as well as an award-winning editor and author of 36 books including *Law Librarianship in the Digital Age* for which she won the AALL's 2014 Joseph L. Andrews Legal Literature Award. Her ten-book technology series, *The Tech Set* won the ALA's Best Book in Library Literature Award in 2011. Ms. Kroski is a librarian, an adjunct faculty member at Drexel and San Jose State University, and an international conference speaker. She was named the winner of the 2017 Library Hi Tech Award from the ALA/LITA for her long-term contributions in the area of Library and Information Science technology and its application.

## Recent Books in the Series Include:

50. *Gaming Programs for All Ages in the Library: A Practical Guide for Librarians* by Tom Bruno

51. *Intentional Marketing: A Practical Guide for Librarians* by Carol Ottolenghi

# Library Management
## A Practical Guide for Librarians

**Bridgit McCafferty**

PRACTICAL GUIDES FOR LIBRARIANS, NO. 77

ROWMAN & LITTLEFIELD
*Lanham • Boulder • New York • London*

Published by Rowman & Littlefield
An imprint of The Rowman & Littlefield Publishing Group, Inc.
4501 Forbes Boulevard, Suite 200, Lanham, Maryland 20706
www.rowman.com

6 Tinworth Street, London SE11 5AL, United Kingdom

British Library Cataloguing in Publication Information Available

**Library of Congress Cataloging-in-Publication Data**

Names: McCafferty, Bridgit, 1984- author.
Title: Library management : a practical guide for librarians / Bridgit
   McCafferty.
Description: Lanham : Rowman & Littlefield, [2021] | Series: Practical
   guides for librarians ; 77 | Includes bibliographical references and
   index. | Summary: "This practical guide explores the different
   managerial roles at libraries, looking at the levels of managers, what
   they do, and how they do it. The book will help prepare early and
   mid-career librarians to step into new roles"—Provided by publisher.
Identifiers: LCCN 2020054931 (print) | LCCN 2020054932 (ebook) | ISBN
   9781538144619 (paperback) | ISBN 9781538144626 (epub)
Subjects: LCSH: Library administrators. | Library administration. | Project
   management. | Leadership.
Classification: LCC Z682.4.A34 M39 2021  (print) | LCC Z682.4.A34  (ebook)
   | DDC 025.1—dc23
LC record available at https://lccn.loc.gov/2020054931
LC ebook record available at https://lccn.loc.gov/2020054932

This book is dedicated to my husband, Justin, and our two darling children, Owen and Clara. They remind me every day of what is most important in life.

# Contents

**Part III: Upper Management**

# Preface

This book is the culmination of eight years of experience learning the job as a director, and then dean, of libraries at a small regional institution. Like many directors, I became an administrator, not by design but by accident. A supervisor left unexpectedly, and I was asked to fill in as an interim director. This was an especially difficult role to assume because the university was, at that time, going through initial accreditation and separating from its parent institution, including licensing for a brand-new digital library and building a library facility. This book is the result of this experience, both during my time as an interim director and then as a permanent director and dean. The topics covered include those that I found most mystifying or challenging in those first months after my appointment.

This book takes a practical approach. There are many excellent works about library management, and this is not an attempt reinvent the wheel. Rather, I try to take a more hands-on, less formal, view of the topic for those who are thrown, like I was, into a new position and need to learn as they go. One particular focus is soft or localized skills that directors usually learn on the job. Each section of the book provides a myriad of examples, many from within libraries and some from outside of libraries, to help readers understand the content. Examples are often taken from real-life situations, though anonymized or changed enough so they aren't identifiable when they relate to sensitive topics. Where relevant, this volume cites other works that provide more theoretical or technical information than could be covered here. *Library Management 101* by Lisa K. Hussey and Diane Velasquez (2019) is a handy volume, and this book tries to augment the information these authors provide, rather than repeat it.

This book is divided into three parts: project management, middle management, and upper management. These cover the different kinds of challenges that face people at each level of their career, exploring how these challenges can help prepare librarians for promotion to the next level. Their purpose is to show how management skills develop over the course of one's career, and to explore how leaders change from context to context. Though each part focuses on a particular level of authority, the lessons can be useful for and applied to all of the levels discussed. For instance, there is a chapter about organizational culture for middle managers that could also be useful for directors. The chapter on group development is a precursor to working with all sorts of groups, including work teams. These are just a few examples. Each chapter builds on, refines, and expands the content presented before it.

The ideal reader for this book is a new librarian or middle manager who wants to understand the competencies required for, and issues faced at, each level of leadership, as well as how different types of professional experiences can help them progress in their career toward director. This should act as a basic introduction to these topics, which are often covered in more depth elsewhere.

## References

Hussey, Lisa K., and Diane L. Velasquez, eds. 2019. *Library Management 101: A Practical Guide.* Chicago: ALA Editions. Kindle.

# PROJECT MANAGEMENT

# The Role of the Project Manager

Plans are worthless, but planning is everything.
—DWIGHT D. EISENHOWER (BLAIR 1957)

PROJECT MANAGEMENT IS THE ACT OF MAKING A PLAN, and then working through everything that inevitably goes wrong as it is pursued. The point is to think through various contingencies, rather than to prescribe exactly how the project will proceed. General Dwight D. Eisenhower, one of the planners behind the 1944 D-Day invasion, knew this as well as anyone. Many problems arose during the landings, resulting in a catastrophic loss of life on the beaches of Normandy (Tucker-Jones 2019). The Allies succeeded despite these setbacks because they were quick to adapt to the situation on the ground, including the changing weather and the opening for attack this provided. Though the objectives for the first day of the landing were not met, the detailed process of planning ensured success over many days, allowing a slow expansion of territory (Tucker-Jones 2019). By planning through each contingency, the D-Day leaders could adapt to new situations with a clear idea of what needed to happen next—after all, the time to think through alternate routes is not in the middle of the catastrophe. Though this bit of history makes project management seem like an exercise in futility, what it really demonstrates is the reality of leading a team. Leaders at every level must understand how to make a plan, but also how to change course when situations go south. This is the great strength of a good project manager.

Leading short-term initiatives in libraries is a stepping stone toward mid-level supervisory roles because, through project management, early-career librarians learn how to plan and how to adapt. This is true for small and large projects, from a few days of shelf shifting to setting up a new integrated library system. Each project carries with it lessons about how to manage complications, both interpersonal and logistical. Project management is the best way to learn the soft skills that lead to a permanent position as a library manager later in a career.

Throughout this part of the book, a project manager is defined as a leader of a group for the purpose of a short- or long-term assignment, but not a permanent supervisor. This type of role, both formal and informal, is common in libraries and provides experience with a variety of managerial competencies, including mediating between group members, allocating resources, formulating assessment measures, and motivating others to achieve a goal. While the lack of direct, supervisory authority can make the role particularly difficult, since it means that problem team members can't be disciplined directly, it also makes for a better leader who is more focused on positive, rather than negative, motivation. In fact, project management teaches future leaders that each person responds differently to assorted drives, and that encouraging individuals requires a variety of approaches from person to person, and even from day to day.

Similarly, leading projects teaches those in early career or with little management experience how to organize the effort of others. Though this may seem like a straightforward proposition, people are not uniform in the way they work. This includes the pace, approach, and quality with which they complete tasks. When managers make mistakes in this regard, they usually overmanage or undermanage. If they overmanage, it is called micromanaging, where supervisors try to control every aspect of someone's work. If they undermanage, it's called a laissez-faire management style, which means that managers give little input to those on their team. Either approach is generally unproductive, and impacts morale. The reality is that there will always be employees who work differently than the leader, and learning how to direct them in a low-stakes situation like a small project can save managers from problems down the line when they have to supervise a similar employee full-time. When a project is over, a colleague goes back to being a colleague, but an employee remains an employee until their job changes or they separate from the institution. Figuring out the best approach in a temporary situation helps prevent long-lasting problems when later situations are not.

Another difficulty of project management is that members of the team may have positions in the larger institution that put them above the project leader in the day-to-day hierarchy of authority. A common instance of this is when a younger librarian leads a committee with more senior staff. Let's say the committee is tasked with creating a new collection development policy. This committee includes department heads from various units across the library, since it impacts multiple areas. The young librarian must learn how to approach these more experienced members of the team with both authority and deference. That can be challenging, since she has to take the lead without stepping on any toes.

This scenario might not seem directly relevant to the role of a middle manager, but actually it is a key to success at this level. Though people often think about middle managers as supervisors, they are really mediators before they are anyone's boss. This is to say that, while they manage others, the real hallmark of their role in the library is that they are sandwiched between the administration and the rest of the library staff. The job is, fundamentally, negotiating between those they report to and those who report to them. Being able to work with more experienced librarians who have more authority, and especially showing confidence in leading a group with such members, can train early-career librarians to navigate the liminal space between administration and staff that mid-level managers occupy. Their role requires the ability to hold two identities at once, that of a colleague and that of an administrator. Acting in the role of a leader in the context of the team, though one might be a junior librarian, can help to understand this frame of mind prior to entering middle management.

Equally as important is learning to think of oneself as an authority in libraries, even when speaking to people who are further up in the management structure. Leading teams of more experienced librarians develops this ability. Library administrators must earn the respect of those above them in order to ensure their judgement is trusted when matters relevant to the library are discussed. A director who isn't consulted about a new facility or a potential major cut to the budget isn't very effective, especially if the reason they aren't consulted is a lack of confidence in their judgement. Administrators have to be the library expert in the room, and they have to be trusted in that capacity, even when they are talking to a mayor or university president. Though these high-stakes interactions may not seem at all related to a collection development policy overhaul, the same strategies for establishing competence and authority are effective in both settings. Getting past the imposter syndrome and learning to trust one's own instincts is the first step, and little projects can help significantly.

Project management also trains potential leaders to take responsibility for the accomplishment of goals, while deflecting praise to members of the team. As an individual contributor, librarians aren't accountable for the work of others. Managers are. They have to take responsibility for meeting deadlines and making progress, even when their employees are the reason for failure. Conversely, when the team is commended, good managers don't accept the praise as though success was solely theirs, but instead point to how staff contributed. If the cataloger colleague of an acquisitions librarian makes a mistake, the acquisitions librarian likely won't take the blame for that mistake. That is, unless they are on a team where the acquisitions librarian is the project manager, and the team misses a due date because of the cataloger's mistake. In this case, as the leader, the acquisitions librarian should take responsibility. When the team succeeds, the acquisitions librarian, as the lead, should give credit to the cataloger and all of the other team members who helped. That's what a team lead does, but it is particularly difficult, especially when things go wrong due to someone else's negligence. Learning how to handle these situations with grace takes time and practice.

In addition to these soft skills, project managers learn how to do assessment. Mid- and upper-level administrators spend an inordinate amount of time on assessment, and those with a knack for it will likely do well in these kinds of roles. On the other hand, those who hate assessment probably won't fit well in the upper administration of a library. Assessment is how library administrators make decisions, allocate resources, and show impact to stakeholders that determine the future of the library. While it can seem like busywork, assessment is the fuel in the engine that makes everything else go. Administrators who don't understand it, or don't use it to make decisions, are working without guideposts. This has a direct impact on the success of the library, and on the morale of staff, who will feel like they are not being led with forethought and intention. Assessment is also a first exposure to compliance. People who like assessment will probably also understand financial accountability, legal liability, and a host of other topics to which administrators are beholden, even when they make life more difficult or throw up roadblocks for new initiatives. Many people actively detest assessment, and for them, administration is likely to be a chore.

This final point exposes the most important insight that project management can provide to early-career librarians: whether or not becoming a supervisor is for them. At some point in any professional career, it feels like the next natural step is to move into management. The problem with this is that management isn't for everyone. While fantasizing about being the dean might while away some slow hours at the reference desk, the reality is far from the fantasy. The truth is that, for every morning a dean walks in the front door of the library feeling like the leader who has it all together, there are ten mornings where she sneaks up the back stairs to avoid getting asked questions about staplers and printers before she's had her morning coffee. Taking responsibility for other people's mistakes can be frustrating, and being accountable for their livelihoods is anxiety causing. Some people are inscrutable, and managing them is a daily struggle. There will never be enough resources for the library, even though the new lazy river at the rec center just got its seventh facelift, and about once a year, there's a good chance the dean has to call the police. There is a reason that reference librarians are some of the longest-lived professionals, and why library deans are not.

This is all to say that one of the best reasons to manage projects before becoming a mid-level supervisor is that management isn't for everyone, and while taking on a temporary initiative is short-lived, permanently switching jobs is not. The worst situation is to switch into management only to learn that it isn't a good fit. Keep in mind that some people are great leaders without ever becoming supervisors. There isn't a single road. Project management is the best way to find out that the expected next step is not the right next step. As General Eisenhower said, "plans are worthless." Learning how to plan, and how to lead in the way that makes the best sense for the individual, is everything.

## References

Blair, William M. 1957. "President Draws Planning Moral: Recalls Army Days to Show Value of Preparedness in Time of Crisis." *New York Times*, November 15. ProQuest Historical New York Times.

Tucker-Jones, Anthony. 2019. *D-Day 1944: The Making of Victory*. Gloucestershire, UK: The History Press. EBSCO eBook Collection.

# Leadership Styles

WHAT MAKES A GOOD LEADER? That's a question that the best administrators must return to at regular intervals, and the answer can change across a career. For a practical examination of management, a chapter about the theories underpinning leadership styles may seem oddly placed, but this question is the heart of this chapter, and really, the heart of the entire book. These theories are simply ways of understanding leadership, and especially, what approach makes a good leader. This is all to say that administrators must know, for themselves, the kind of manager they want to be. They should be intentional in the way they comport themselves, to ensure they attempt to live up to their own ideals. That is what this chapter is about, in a practical sense: exploring effective and ineffective ways a leader can act.

## Definitions

Leadership style: The approach someone takes when serving in a management role.

## What Makes a Good Leader?

Before looking at management styles, a better understanding of the broader question of good leadership is necessary. A manager's personal sense of what makes him or her effective significantly impacts how that manager performs the role, and can be a guidepost to return to again and again when tough decisions are required. Some people prize innovation and adaptability, others value bravery in the pursuit of what must be done, and still others believe that leaders make mistakes and learn from them. Each of these views holds a kernel of truth, and reveals something about the nature of leadership. Whatever one's personal philosophy happens to be, the unifying thread is that good leaders think about leadership, and their own approach to it. Often, they view it through the prism of their personal experiences, both successes and failures.

There is no one answer to the question "what makes a good leader?" that is going to satisfy every person or sum up the best philosophy in each case. Every profession, including librarianship, needs a variety of leaders with a multitude of approaches to keep it vital. Different kinds of leaders challenge one another and ensure that the good work that needs doing is done. They each act as an innovator in tackling one or a few in the host of problems, and train others to carry on their work.

That said, throughout this book, discussions of leadership are built on a belief that some of the best library managers are authentic in the way they guide others, even when they make mistakes, which is a belief taken from Sheryl Sandberg, the current COO of Facebook (2013). Moreover, the philosophy of leadership presented here is underpinned by a simple, unofficial motto that once famously belonged to Google: "don't be evil" (Conger 2018). In other words, good librarians do good. They do the right thing, as they understand it. This is, after all, a profession and industry predicated on the central tenet of helping people.

Ultimately, the best way to lead in any given situation is up to individual managers, based on their personality, the context in which they work, and their goals. This is where leadership styles become important.

## ◎ Leadership Styles

A leadership style is the method someone uses when serving in a management role. These styles describe a person's approach based on their actions, personality traits, environment, communications style, and decision-making process. By understanding leadership styles, managers can be intentional in the way they make choices, and can appreciate the strengths and weaknesses that their chosen style offers. This also ensures that, when necessary, managers are able to adapt. Though most people lean toward one style or another, certain challenges lend themselves to different tactics. The best leaders are flexible; they switch as needed. No one leadership approach works in every situation and with every group of people. For this reason, knowing the styles of leadership, and their usefulness, is important.

The concept of leadership styles was first proposed by Kurt Lewin in the 1930s. Lewin and his colleagues Ronald Lippitt and Ralph K. White identified three basic styles. Most other theories derive from this original classification:

- Authoritarian: A leader who makes decisions without consulting others. The benefit is that decisions are made quickly. The drawback is that employees become easily demoralized when their input is not considered nor sought.
- Democratic: A leader who makes decisions after consulting with their team. This is much better for staff morale, but decisions take longer because quality input requires time.
- Laissez-faire: A leader who gives minimal feedback to their employees, and remains hands off when it comes to day-to-day decision-making and activities. Employees benefit from a great deal of autonomy, but they can feel adrift without any clear direction from management (Lewin, Lippit, and White 1939).

Over the years, this list of leadership styles was expanded to include both approaches to leadership and types of leaders. This concept also changed to recognize that, as mentioned above, effective leaders don't use only one style. Though many people have a single overarching approach they prefer, there is no way to truly "know your leadership style," because it is not immutable. The best managers employ the right style, at the right time. This makes a manager more effective, by helping to negate some of the negative aspects of the preferred style.

## Primal Leadership

In *Primal Leadership*, Daniel Goleman, Richard Boyatzis, and Annie McKee (2013) expanded on leadership style, suggesting that emotional intelligence enables the best leaders to succeed. They proposed six types of leaders based on different types of emotional intelligence, which form the core of many modern lists of leadership styles. These include:

- Visionary: Visionary leaders focus on defining a unifying goal. They allow their team to come up with strategies to reach this objective. Visionary leaders often prize innovation, and accept the failures that sometimes come along with trying new approaches. A visionary style is handy for libraries in need of change.
- Coaching: This style focuses on the goals of employees. Coaching managers support team members by helping them build on strengths to grow and succeed. This style is useful with employees who are inexperienced, early career, or need motivation.
- Affiliative: These leaders make connections and create relationships that lead to a well-functioning team. This works well in situations where the team has negative conflict, or there are divisions.
- Democratic: Democratic leaders are consensus builders. They look to the team to determine the best way to act and how to reach goals. This style is useful when a leader is not as knowledgeable as other team members, or where members have specific, relevant expertise related to the problem. This is also useful when the team is made of colleagues, rather than subordinates, since the focus is on collaboration.
- Pacesetting: These leaders set hard-to-reach goals and hold team members strictly accountable for these goals. This is valuable when the team has aggressive, short-term objectives, but it does not work well over the long term because of burnout and impact on morale. Team members should be rewarded and shown immense appreciation if this style is employed.
- Commanding: Commanding leaders are often viewed in a negative light. They lead through fear or strict adherence to the rules. They are autocratic, and most effective in crisis situations where immediate control is necessary. This is not usually effective, since team members are likely to be resistant (Goleman, Boyatzis, and McKee 2013).

The primary thesis of *Primal Leadership* is that managers must act with emotional intelligence, because working at a place is more than just doing prescribed tasks in a certain way toward a defined goal (Goleman, Boyatzis, and McKee 2013). Leadership means setting a climate and shaping the experience people have when they are at work. In other words, how people feel about the job they do is important. When employees care about their library and occupation, they work more, and better. These leadership styles significantly impact the emotional aspect of the employee experience.

Though many interviews for management positions ask "what is your leadership style?" no one will have a set style, a point discussed often in *Primal Leadership* (Goleman, Boyatzis, and McKee 2013). A new library director may need to be visionary when starting a position to effect change in the organization and realize their goals, distinct from those of their predecessor. As time goes on, this leader might fall back into more of a coaching role, helping new staff or early-career librarians. Once the staff meets the aspirations of the leader, and gains a high degree of competence, the library director may default to a democratic leadership style, which is especially useful with an experienced, professional staff. During this time there may be moments of pacesetting in advance of significant deadlines, such as the beginning of a summer reading program or an accreditation review. There may also be the occasional crisis, necessitating a more commanding style as the library recovers. As this example suggests, though some of these styles may have a negative reputation, each has its purpose and place.

One thing to remember is that, when someone describes their leadership style, they are often telegraphing who they want to be, not necessarily who they are. These styles are extraordinarily aspirational. Not everyone is going to succeed at being a visionary leader in every instance, and with every employee. There are people who simply don't want to participate in this type of leadership experience. Good leaders understand the limits of theory, and use these "styles" to think about the possibilities in their own leadership, and to strive to be more than just someone who tells other people what to do. A person might be a great leader in certain situations, and middling or substandard in others, simply because they were naturally suited to a set of circumstances where they were called on to make a difference.

This was the case for Clara Barton, as an example. She was the founder of the American Red Cross, and a leader of nurses on the battlefield during the Civil War. She could move badly needed supplies to the front, and keep her cool in exceedingly dangerous situations. She had an incredible passion for healing soldiers, despite great personal risk. She is considered the mother of modern, professional nursing. She served as the president of the American Red Cross for its first 23 years, but eventually was forced out of this role. The authoritarian approach to leadership that was so effective in the crisis situation of a battlefield, was not conducive to managing a vast and rapidly growing nonprofit at the beginning of the twentieth century. The organization asked her to step down when it determined that a democratic approach was a better fit, one to which she could not adapt (Burton 1995).

There are two lessons here. The first is that even the authoritarian style, which gets such a bad rap today, has its place, and its purpose. There are times when it is the only effective way to lead a group through a disaster. The second is that even a truly visionary leader can succeed in one context, and fail in another, due to an inability to adapt. That said, despite this late-in-life failure, Barton's incredible bravery and deep passion for her cause, as well as her willingness to do the right thing in the most difficult of circumstances, is what made her great. The organization she founded has helped millions of people through the worst moments of their lives. Compared to this, her management style is an afterthought. This is to say that people do seem to remember leaders who do the right thing, far more than those who simply do things right.

## ⊚ Key Points

- There are many ways to define good leadership. Whether or not a leader is successful is largely contextual and dependent on personality traits, situational factors, and goals.

- Leadership styles can help managers think about how they lead, and improve.
- Leadership styles may change over the course of a career, usually in response to the given needs of a management position.

## References

Burton, David H. 1995. *Clara Barton: In the Service of Humanity*. Westport, CT: Praeger. EBSCO eBook Collection.

Conger, Kate. 2018. "Google Removes 'Don't Be Evil' Clause from Its Code of Conduct." *Gizmodo*, May 18. https://gizmodo.com/google-removes-nearly-all-mentions-of-dont-be-evil-from-1826153393.

Goleman, Daniel, Richard Boyatzis, and Annie McKee. 2013. *Primal Leadership*. Boston: Harvard Business School Press. Kindle.

Lewin, Kurt, Ronald Lippitt, and Ralph K. White. 1939. "Patterns of Aggressive Behavior in Experimentally Created 'Social Climates.'" *Journal of Social Psychology* 10: 271–99. Taylor & Francis Online.

Sandberg, Sheryl. 2013. *Lean In: Women, Work, and the Will to Lead*. New York: Alfred K. Knopf. Kindle.

# Group Development and Conflict

WHEN GROUPS WORK WELL TOGETHER, nothing is better. The give and take between members as they push each other to achieve more can be intensely productive. Some of the best, most satisfying work comes from really effective teams. People often reminisce about their success and comradery even years after the project ends. Conversely, groups that are working poorly can feel like a giant chore. The almost universal hatred of group assignments is a direct result of experiences with low-functioning teams forced together in school. Everyone has that one memory of staying up late to do all of the work for a group that simply couldn't pull it together. These kinds of groups give all the rest a bad name.

The project manager has a significant role to play in ensuring that groups are functioning as they should. To be successful in this regard, project managers need to understand the stages of group development, and the role they play in determining the ultimate success of the group. This is because some stages that are pivotal to group development will also feel turbulent and fraught. High-functioning groups often feature robust debate among members about disagreements, while underperforming teams may never have a single dispute. A project manager who understands these stages, and the importance of constructive conflict, can navigate the difficult times and reassure other group members that, despite the turmoil, the group is still on track.

Keep in mind that there are plenty of teams that seem headed for disaster just as they are about to achieve incredible success. Members must trust one another enough to challenge ideas and contribute honestly. This active debate and consensus-building is what leads to the most productive teams. John Lennon and Paul McCartney, one of the most successful songwriting teams of all time, are a duo that exemplifies this concept. They were different in their approaches, and their musical styles were often divergent. They challenged one another, pushing each other to fix problems and write better (Bonner 2020). This conflict, and the iterative process of improving one another's songs that resulted from it, led to exceptional music. The trust they had for one another enabled them to voice criticism and disagreements when needed.

This same principle works with other kinds of groups. The best work doesn't occur when everyone gets along—it is produced by the honest exchange of ideas, through a repeating process of improvement. Groupthink, or the tendency to force members to conform to the prevalent thought processes within a group, is not helpful, though it feels comfortable when everyone agrees. For this reason, one of the most important people in the group is also the one that causes the most conflict. This person is called the devil's advocate. The purpose of the devil's advocate is to question the decisions of the group, and to point out issues with the plan arrived at through the consensus of other members. Though the impulse of others is often to silence those who detract from the coherence and harmony, a devil's advocate is actually an essential group member who pushes others to perform better.

Because people are hard-wired to experience disagreements as bad or wrong, the group leader has to know how conflict functions in group dynamics, and how to guide groups through it. Part of this is understanding how groups develop. Part of it is knowing which kinds of conflict are productive, and which are unproductive, as well as the true hallmarks and causes of dysfunctional teams. When leaders can identify if groups are functioning as expected, or if they are misfiring, and why, they can get a project back on track before the situation reaches a crisis mode. More importantly, leaders who understand these concepts can act as a firm hand, reassuring other group members when productive conflict seems like it might overwhelm the group.

As an example, a committee chair working to hire a new head of technical services might find that the members are at cross-purposes due to strong support for an internal candidate by some, and deep distrust of the same candidate by others. This is a productive conflict that can be shaped to create a healthy dialogue about the type of technical services head that should be hired. A chair who doesn't understand models of group development may handle the conflict as though it is unproductive, trying to quiet dissent rather than allowing the conversation to develop. A chair who understands group development will reassure concerned committee members, and guide the group toward a positive resolution of the search. In a practical sense, these concepts really matter!

## Definitions

Constructive conflict: Conflict that results in growth, problem solving, increased involvement, and greater cohesion through a robust consensus-building process.

Destructive conflict: Conflicts that result in a lack of resolution to problems.

Devil's advocate: A group member who points out weaknesses or argues against the dominant thinking of the group in order to ensure problems are adequately addressed.

Dysfunctional team: A team that does not reach its goals due to problems with group dynamics.

Groupthink: The tendency to force members to conform to the dominant thought processes within a group.

Systems theory: A theory of social systems that explains how members of groups form alliances, create relationships, and interact based on the larger sets of beliefs, values, attitudes, and experiences that shape the way they view others.

## Models of Group Development

Models of group development endeavor to explore how groups form, complete a task, and dissolve by systematically analyzing group dynamics. Kurt Lewin, mentioned in the last chapter, first coined the term "group dynamics" to describe the way teams interact and work together (1947). Based on the work of Lewin and others, Bruce Tuckman developed his stages model of group development (1965). This became the most influential theory of group development, and is the basis for most other related theories, though many change the elements of each stage. Tuckman's model has five stages: forming, storming, norming, performing, and adjourning (Tuckman and Jensen 1977). These are the phases that each group moves through as it works toward a goal.

Tuckman describes the stages of group development as follows:

- Forming: The stage where members are unfamiliar with one another. They are getting acquainted, and as a result, are still polite. Members in this stage are hesitant to speak up, since they are still learning about others in the group.
- Storming: The group moves into productive activities. In order to begin the project, the group must establish protocols, communication channels, decision-making strategies, and subgroups. This stage is rife with conflict because group members challenge one another in order to figure out the power structures. This makes storming uncomfortable.
- Norming: At this point, the rules underpinning how the group does business are established and expectations for members are defined. The group often forms its own unique culture during this phase.
- Performing: The group does the actual work with which it has been tasked. If forming, storming, and norming have succeeded, the group is now functional, with shared goals. At this point, individual group members are performing to a high degree.
- Adjourning: The group has finished its work. Group members receive recognition of their achievements, and take time to reminisce about what they have accomplished before going their separate ways (Tuckman and Jensen 1977).

One approach to understanding these stages is to think of a heist movie, like *Ocean's 11*. A group is brought together, each with unique talents. They face some disagreements, but ultimately all become buddies. They pull off a major, previously unthinkable heist, and then stand outside the Bellagio, sad to see it end but proud of what they've achieved. All teams go through these same stages, not just groups of internationally renowned thieves.

For this reason, it is essential to understand each stage. First, leaders who understand these stages know how to nurture their team throughout the process. Second, leaders who understand the stages know how to avoid the pitfalls of each, and how the stages contribute to the overall functioning of the team. This is especially true in a phase like storming, which can feel like the group will never come together due to the inherent conflict involved in creating norms. Leaders who understand that this is a natural step have a better sense of where the group is headed than leaders who don't.

The first stage, forming, might seem straightforward, but this is a point where the leader is especially crucial. The most important opportunity given to team members during the forming stage is the chance to get to know one another, and to create a cohesive, mutual understanding of mission and goals. This shared sense of purpose helps the group move through the next stage, storming, because it is unifying, even when conflict seems unending. Other important work that occurs during this stage includes setting timelines, creating budgets, gathering resources, divvying up tasks, and establishing regular meetings. The leader is key to navigating each of these discussions because the group members are hesitant to join in, since they don't know the others on the team. They are still in the "polite" phase where no one wants to step on toes. The leader is required to set the agenda and ensure that decisions are made with input from the group.

To understand forming a little better, think of a common project encountered by libraries, the renovation of a library facility. During a renovation project, a library would typically have a committee working to provide input and determine what the library will look like after. During the forming stage, this committee needs to know the basic information: how much money is allocated, who is on the team, how long will the project take, why is it happening, and what is the goal. The leader of the committee has these details, whereas others probably don't. This type of committee is also likely made up of library staff from different departments and levels of management. These staff members might not have a lot of experience working with one another, so the librarian in charge needs to help everyone become better acquainted. The purpose of this stage is to simply set the parameters of the project as it goes forward, and make sure that the main goals are understood by everyone on the team.

The next stage is storming. This is where the more divisive decisions, guidelines, expectations, and dynamics of the group are established. Storming tends to feel uncomfortable, but it is necessary because every group has disruptive decisions to make before it can do its best work. By the storming phase, the group members who have stronger, more assertive personalities emerge, as well as those who are reserved. Also, by this phase, group members understand their shared mission and have a commitment to success. This commitment makes the end product vital to members, which leads to a greater willingness during the storming phase to challenge the ideas and contributions of others in order to ensure the best outcomes possible. This impulse to confront causes tension between different types of group members, and may raise tough questions, such as how will people be rewarded for individual contributions, who has authority to make decisions, and what responsibilities each team member will have. These can be contentious, as they are not as clear-cut as the questions raised during forming, which tend to be about the overarching mission and goals of the project. If group formation is a heist movie, storming is the scene where it all seems sure to fail—but that doesn't mean this phase should be avoided! Every group must go through storming in order to work out the problematic issues that are bound to arise. Leaders who understand that this is a normal, natural part of group development can help navigate it by guiding conversations and reminding group members who feel discouraged that this is how the process should work.

Returning to the example of a committee overseeing a library renovation, the storming phase is likely to be rife with conflict. A library renovation, more than almost any other project that takes place in a library, results in winners and losers. This is because of difficult decisions about whether space is given to the children's section or the computer lab, whether the stacks are going to lose some of their footprint, or the catalogers their offices. These are tough decisions. Storming, in this context, is going to be difficult because everyone is going to have an interest in getting the right resources for their respective areas, which may mean arguing against resources for others. During storming, a leader is going to be most useful in mediating these difficult discussions, and especially reminding group members that the goal is to refresh the library facility in a way that works best for patrons.

Leaders should make sure that each group member is heard during these difficult discussions, and that ways of making decisions and guiding principles in decision-making are established appropriately with input from the whole group. If there are two or three members who seem to be especially confrontational, the leader might even pull them aside to mediate a resolution between them outside of the normal group communication. For instance, having the children's librarian and the technology supervisor determine in private what each needs versus wants, and how these needs can be met for both, might decrease discord for the larger group. Having the group start with small or less contentious decisions, such as the type of furniture to buy, might be one way to establish protocols that help later on for more difficult decisions. Also keep in mind that group members don't know one another well during the storming phase, so activities that focus on how members of the group communicate can be helpful in working through some of the strife.

The next phase, norming, is the stage where questions raised in storming are answered, and the group is able to settle into the processes of working together. When groups reach the norming stage, members feel more comfortable communicating with one another. They understand how other team members interact, and feel free to discuss problems and concerns, thanks to the progress made during the storming phase. Also thanks to storming, the group is able to work through problems that arise with minimal negative conflict because it has established effective strategies to deal with these situations. During this stage, the leader has a smaller role. A good leader knows how to step back at this point to foster cooperation and problem solving. Group members should take center stage.

For the group working on the library renovation, the norming phase is reached when members are able to resolve conflict without having a serious confrontation. For instance, early on, it might be really difficult to make a decision on the issue of whether to get rid of the technical services offices in favor of a smaller space with cubicles, especially if reducing the number of offices leads to a badly needed bigger footprint for the children's area. Once norming has occurred, the conversation about this is likely to be more productive. The established communication protocols should go a long way toward making sure that opposing sides actually listen to one another. Where technical services may have felt like their needs were being ignored previously, they feel heard now. The leader is less hands-on in this phase, but can help by ensuring these established protocols are followed, and by adjourning the group when things become too heated or unproductive, allowing people time to cool off.

Performing is the "doing" phase. Depending on the project, this is often the most activity-intense point for the individual members of the group. Conversely, the leader is usually least active during performing. By this stage, the individual roles are clear. If the group was formed to complete a specific task, such as creating a grant application, performing is where members actually put pen to paper, edit, and pull the final project together. The group has reached peak productivity by this point, resulting in intense action. Group members also know one another fairly well, and understand how each person is contributing to the overall success of the project. This means that morale is usually high.

Performing results in successful completion of the project, and the group should reach its ultimate goal.

In the example of a library renovation, the performing phase would be the stage where the library is actually in the middle of undergoing renovations. Difficult decisions have been made, and the group is actually doing the work—hiring contractors, ordering furniture, and watching the project come together. This stage is the least hands-on for the leader, who mostly ensures that things are happening according to the timeline and budget. It is helpful for the leader to act as a coordinator at this stage by ensuring that contractors, interior designers, and other professionals are scheduled and coming in the right order.

The final phase, adjourning, is the last stage of group development. This may not seem immediately important to new leaders and, in fact, Tuckman didn't originally include it in his model. Once the task is complete, simply dispersing the team seems like the logical next step. However, after working on a project, team members should celebrate their accomplishments. This stage is important because many people require psychological closure and reflection to feel satisfied with the work they have done. Through adjourning, the group leader can also identify ways in which individual members have grown, as well as lessons learned and best practices that may help others during the next project. In the context of libraries, this means passing on information about how the task was completed so that others can replicate success—in the case of the renovation, this may mean doing a presentation at a conference about the process. It may also mean identifying further work to be completed. For instance, if a group has created a new library collection, the leader from the initial project might hand over the responsibility for ongoing collection development to a librarian who can grow from the new responsibility. Good leaders look for ways to advance their team members, even as projects end.

## @ Group Dynamics

In addition to group development, group dynamics also impact the outcome of a project. Teams are not made up of discrete individuals with no bearing on one another. They are social ecosystems, with individuals relating to one another and reacting to shared experiences, values, and goals. Members often act in their own best interests, whether or not they align with the group as a whole. As a result, coalitions, subgroups, and factions are bound to arise whenever a group forms. Leaders must recognize these dynamics and understand how they impact the overall project.

One useful concept related to the way people interact in groups is systems theory. Systems theory is a psychological model that views human behavior as existing within a larger group or social setting. First developed by Ludwig von Bertalanffy, a biologist, in 1968, this theory explains how members of groups form alliances, create relationships, and interact based on the larger sets of beliefs, values, attitudes, and experiences that shape the way they view others. These systems impact the way a group interacts, especially when conflicts arise.

When considering the social systems of a group, there are some handy questions to ask:

- How does the group communicate?
- What alliances exist?
- What roles do different group members play?

- Is the group open to change, or have members developed groupthink?
- What are the patterns of interaction, especially the negative patterns of interaction?

Once patterns of interaction are established, they are difficult to change—in fact, social systems are generally resistant to change. Project managers who identify dysfunctions early have the best shot at getting the group back on track, before negative patterns are well established.

For instance, a project manager might run into a situation where two group members value radically different aspects of a project that are at odds. Perhaps the goal is to create a new first-year experience course, and a librarian in the group is focused on information literacy, while a career services representative wants to spend more time in the course helping students find jobs after they graduate. They conflict with one another because of their professional backgrounds. Each person has several group members who have taken "their side," and it's clear that neither is willing to cede. In this case a leader would probably pull aside these two members to mediate new ways of dealing with their conflict. This mediation might start with the fact that they are both deeply concerned about what is best for the students, as common ground, and then move to ways of changing negative patterns of interaction once shared values are established.

## ⑥ Dysfunctional Teams

The most well-known model of team dysfunction comes from *The Five Dysfunctions of a Team* by Patrick Lencioni (2002). These are:

- Inattention to results: Group members focus on their own goals or successes, rather than the overall results of the project.
- Avoidance of accountability: Group members don't hold one another responsible, even when standards are not met or are set too low.
- Lack of commitment: Group members are not dedicated to the goals and mission of the team. They lack "buy-in."
- Fear of conflict: Group members self-sensor to keep the peace. Actual, constructive debates are avoided.
- Absence of trust: Group members are not willing to be vulnerable with one another when sharing ideas or criticism, because they don't trust others (Lencioni 2002).

These are common problems in many different types of teams. Notably, Lencioni focuses on conflict as a path to authentic commitment, which is the cornerstone of a successful project (2002). This demonstrates why the conflict stage of Tuckman's (1965) model of group development is so pivotal. Many new leaders think that a group working with relatively little conflict and a high degree of agreement is ideal, though this might actually indicate a group that lacks trust. These groups often silence people with new ideas or who simply don't agree with the dominant opinion—those highly important devil's advocates. This results in a lack of commitment to the group, an unwillingness by members to risk holding others accountable and, potentially, a group that doesn't get results. Conflict is important in group dynamics, though this is counterintuitive. The key is a group leader who can manage, harness, and negotiate conflict toward productive ends.

The first step when managing group conflict is to ensure that the discordance is constructive, rather than destructive, by focusing on the process used to resolve it. This was first proposed in 1973 by Morton Deutsch, who believed conflict can be good for organizations, just as it can be bad. When conflict is resolved constructively, it results in people growing, increased involvement by members, and greater cohesion through a robust consensus-building process. Conversely, conflicts that are resolved through a destructive process result in a lack of resolution to problems. This also distracts group members, and diverts resources from the group's objective. Destructive conflict can impact team morale and divide the group into competing factions (Deutsch 2009).

The goal of a leader is to ensure that conflicts fall into the constructive category. To do this, leaders must promote trust, openness to real debate, commitment to the success of the team, accountability, and the importance of the team's success over the individual contributions of members. As Deutsch suggests, cooperative solutions that are seen as win-win are the key to ensuring conflicts are constructive (2009). Though conflict is necessary for a well-functioning group, members cannot be openly antagonistic to others or unwilling to compromise. These characteristics lead to destructive conflict. In addition to antagonism, the size of conflicts also impacts whether they become destructive—larger conflicts often become destructive, particularly if they are at the center of the project or involve strong value or belief systems that are discordant (Deutsch 2009). Fostering open communication, a willingness to cooperate, and a shared sense of purpose can diminish the potential for destructive conflict.

As Deutsch's theory suggests, the process used to resolve a conflict determines whether it becomes constructive or destructive. To this end, conflict resolution can be a valuable tool to ensure that the group remains productive. One theory of conflict resolution, the Thomas-Kilmann model (Thomas 1988), suggests that there are five potential approaches to resolving conflict, and each approach can be mapped on an axis ranking assertiveness and cooperativeness:

- Avoiding: Ignoring the problem. This ensures there is no solution.
- Accommodating: Ceding one's own concerns in favor of someone else's. This resolves the conflict quickly, but at the expense of one person's point of view. This often leads to resentment.
- Compromising: Settling on a solution where no one gets exactly what they want. This is the best way to make everyone feel mildly pleased with the outcome, but might also result in a poor solution that takes the worst from every proposal.
- Competing: Win-lose. Someone tries to dominate the situation, resulting in the implementation of that person's solution at the expense of others. This is good for situations where an unpopular decision must be made, or where no compromise is possible. This approach may lead to more innovative solutions, but it often creates antagonistic relationships between group members.
- Collaborating: Working together to find a solution that satisfies everyone as much as possible. This amounts to finding a win-win solution, and is often the best approach (Thomas 1988).

By understanding the different approaches, leaders can help group members work toward the best solution.

As all of these models demonstrate, leaders can't avoid conflict, and shouldn't try. Conflict has an important role to play in the formation of a group and the productivity of members. The key to productive conflict is trust. This does not mean falling into one another's arms at a state park to prove that each team member will catch the other. This means making space in the dialogue for everyone, which is the key job of the group leader as any group develops. Sometimes, group leaders must call on people or tolerate unpopular points of view to ensure that each side in the debate is heard. This does not make anyone happy. All factions feel that they are being overlooked in favor of the other, at least at the start. Eventually, though, if the leader can listen well enough, and create enough room for each member to speak, the team does come together, because they trust that they have agency when it matters. Trusting the process allows team members to buy in to the end product, even if it is not the result they originally wanted. If there is one thing a leader needs to understand, it is that sometimes people just want to be heard, even if they are ultimately overruled. Leaders must respect every member of the team enough to give them a voice. This is good for morale, and it is good for the end product. Sometimes, these outlier points of view can save a project from its biggest mistakes and worst ideas. Many great leaders keep a devil's advocate in the chain of command for just this reason.

Remember, this kind of conflict is not only common in groups that pull together for temporary projects. A big part of the job for any middle manager is resolving unproductive conflict, and guiding productive disputes so that they result in the best possible outcome. New middle managers are consistently shocked by how much of their time goes into mediating between conflicting employees. Learning how to create trust between these employees doesn't only solve one conflict; it makes them feel at ease with one another so that they can work out these disputes for themselves. Trust also ensures that when someone sees a bad plan about to take hold or a huge mistake unfolding, they speak up.

## Key Points

- Conflict in groups is productive, because it pushes each member of a group to do their best work.
- Groups develop in stages, commonly defined as forming, storming, norming, performing, and adjourning.
- Group dynamics are social systems, and they are difficult to change once established.
- Conflicts can be constructive or destructive.

## References

Bertalanffy, Ludwig. 2015. *General System Theory: Foundations, Development, Applications*. Revised Edition, New York: George Braziller Inc. Kindle.

Bonner, Michael. 2020. "Paul McCartney Says He Still Consults John Lennon When Writing Songs." *Uncut*, November 12. https://www.uncut.co.uk/features/paul-mccartney-still-consults-john-lennon-128539/.

Deutsch, Morton. 2009. *The Resolution of Conflict: Constructive and Destructive Processes*. Carl Hovland Memorial Lectures Series. New Haven, CT: Yale University Press.

Lencioni, Patrick. 2002. *The Five Dysfunctions of a Team: A Leadership Fable*. San Francisco, CA: Jossey-Bass.

Lewin, Kurt. 1947. "Frontiers in Group Dynamics: Concept, Method and Reality in Social Science; Social Equilibria and Social Change." *Human Relations* 1 (1): 5–41. SAGE.

Thomas, Kenneth W. 1988. "The Conflict-Handling Modes: Toward a More Precise Theory." *Management Communication Theory* 1 (3): 430–36.

Tuckman, Bruce. 1965. "Developmental Sequence in Small Groups." *Psychological Bulletin* 63 (2): 384–99.

Tuckman, Bruce, and Mary Ann Jensen. 1977. "Stages of Small-Group Development Revisited." *Group Organization and Management* 2 (4): 419–27.

# Project Management Frameworks

PROJECT MANAGEMENT FRAMEWORKS are the organizational systems used to structure the discrete and interdependent tasks that make up a project. Each of these frameworks has its strengths and weaknesses. The best project managers understand the differences between them, and can choose the right one for the job at hand. While managers are likely to have an affinity for certain frameworks, depending on their management style, no one choice works in every situation. Kanban, for instance, might appeal to people who are motivated by visual representations of their workflow, whereas lean project management works best for teams tasked with doing a lot with few resources. Though this chapter provides a basic overview of different frameworks, enough has been written about each to fill a small library—take this as an introduction only!

To understand the importance of choosing the right framework, and using that framework to organize the activities required to complete a project, one need only look at the construction of the Hoover Dam, a famous example of the impact project management can have. Despite the fact that this was one of the biggest and most complicated public works projects ever undertaken, it "was completed two years ahead of schedule and under budget" (Kwak et al. 2014, 256). This is especially impressive given that the dam, which weighs more than 6 million tons, was constructed during the Great Depression, a time of economic and political strife. The project was successful because it was one of the first to use modern techniques, including the Gantt chart.

If there is any field that understands the importance of organization, it is librarianship. Project management frameworks bring organization to the chaos of tasks during a large project. They structure and visualize these activities to keep team members focused on what needs to happen next, and to ensure that interdependencies are considered, so they don't hold up the rest of the work. As the Hoover Dam example shows, even projects with everything working against them are improved by applying a well-thought-through management framework that organizes tasks and ensures cohesion and adaptability by group members.

## Definitions

Brooks's law: More manpower only makes late projects later, because of the time required to bring new team members on board and to communicate their role within the project.

Gantt chart: A visualization of project tasks that outlines which tasks can take place concurrently; which are dependent on other, earlier tasks; and when these tasks need to be completed.

Gold plating: Spending time working on a project when the return on the investment of time is not worth the gain in quality.

Kanban board: A board that categorizes tasks required for project completion in order to facilitate work on the project by group members.

Man-month: The amount of work one employee can complete in a month.

Milestones: Important markers on project timelines that define major project phases.

Slack time: The extra time that a task can take without delaying the project's completion.

Sprint: A short period of time in Agile project management in which the group completes a limited number of tasks.

## 🌀 Basis of Project Management Frameworks

The idea that projects are best managed through plans that map out tasks, deliverables, due dates, and other steps toward completion is an old one. Henry Gantt, famous for his Gantt chart, is often considered the founder of modern project management. The concept of the Gantt chart, used in the construction of the Hoover Dam, debuted in 1917. The Gantt chart is a visualization of project tasks that outlines which can take place concurrently; which are dependent on other, earlier tasks; and when these tasks need to be completed. They are drawn with dates across the top, and activities included as lines spanning the period of time when they need to occur. These charts often have symbols to mark dependencies and milestone due dates.

In the 1950s, many companies developed new methods to manage projects. The goal was to save the company money and use resources efficiently. This included the Critical Path approach to project management, which was developed by DuPont to help plan for factory closures during routine maintenance based on the activities that were least flexible. The Program Evaluation Review Technique (PERT) was also developed in the 1950s by the U.S. Navy to help estimate how long projects would take to complete based on the shortest length of time possible for each task.

Through the 1960s, project management underwent a process of professionalization, and eventually became a career of its own, though many people tasked with managing projects have no formal training. Modern project management frameworks and methodologies focus on estimating the amount of time a project will take based on the tasks required, with a focus on completion in as short amount of time as possible.

These frameworks are grounded in the concept of project life cycle, or the stages a project moves through to reach completion. These phases are:

- Initiation: Finding out about the project. This includes goals, potential for failure, deadlines, deliverables, and other basic details about the project.
- Planning: This is where the tasks are outlined, project plans are created, and responsibilities are assigned.
- Implementation: The actual completion of the work. The plan is executed.
- Closure: The task is finished. Goals are satisfied. The group agrees to dissolve.

Notably, this mirrors the group development cycles presented in the last chapter, which is to say that there are many lenses through which this concept can be understood. These life-cycle phases define the basic structure of a project, with tasks that fall in each part, and that must be completed before another is started.

In addition to life-cycle considerations, project management frameworks also look at the tasks that a project manager must complete to keep the project progressing appropriately. These include ongoing control of the budget and project deadlines. Management frameworks often recommend mechanisms to monitor these aspects as the project moves forward. For instance, in the Agile methodology, managers hold regular—often daily—check-in meetings to stay apprised of task completion. Though these activities happen throughout the course of a project, some descriptions of project life cycles include control and management as a specific life-cycle step between implementation and closure. Others wrap control and management into each part, and especially into the implementation phase.

Project management frameworks also provide apparatuses that managers can use to track the project. The Gantt chart is one example of this. These are tools that leaders can repurpose to meet their own needs as they organize activities. They are often charts, calendars, visualizations of tasks, and other templates. Some project management frameworks have formal, strict tools that practitioners are expected to use, while some are flexible. For instance, the visualization of tasks used in Kanban is quite adaptable—it is just sticky notes on a whiteboard! Other frameworks, such as PRINCE2, are rather rigid about the tools provided.

Please note that many project management frameworks are designed for processes and industries that are different than libraries in important ways. Agile, for instance, was created to aid the development of software, and the Critical Path method was developed to manage and schedule the downtime involved in routine maintenance at chemical plants. As a result, they may need to be adapted to the library setting in order to be the most beneficial for project managers. Some excellent books have been written about project management frameworks related to libraries, including Barbara Allan's *The No-Nonsense Guide to Project Management* (2017) and Carly Wiggins Searcy's *Project Management in Libraries: On Time, On Budget, On Target* (2018).

# ⊚ Types of Project Management Frameworks

Generally, when people discuss project management frameworks, they are referring to a specific type of project management: Agile, for instance, or Scrum. Those who study project management usually group these as methods, methodologies, and frameworks. There is a great deal of debate about what falls into each category, but generally methods are a way of doing some specific management task, such as a Gantt chart. Methodologies are strict and prescriptive ways to approach project management that outline definite steps to take, whereas frameworks are more flexible suggestions that can be implemented based on the context. Each of the approaches discussed here falls into one of these categories. Frameworks are currently the most popular because of their flexibility.

The distinction between rigid and flexible approaches is probably the biggest way to denote different styles. More rigid methodologies have the benefit of ensuring specific goals are met by hard deadlines, whereas the more flexible frameworks don't always ensure that projects are completed in an identified timeframe, but they do allow for adaptability as the project develops. The needs of a project are central when choosing the type of approach to take.

## Common Frameworks

Common frameworks used for project management, and which might be helpful in libraries, are listed below. They mostly come from the private sector, though a few are from government organizations. Many of them were first used in software development. Leaders should consider the degree of flexibility and open-ended-ness of the project when trying to identify the best style to use:

- Waterfall: If someone who had never before worked with project management decided to design a system for it, they might come up with Waterfall. This is the most traditional type of approach. Waterfall involves the sequential ordering of project tasks, placing those tasks into phases. When one phase ends, another begins. This system is good if the tasks are straightforward, or linear, and the end point is clearly defined. Waterfall is not suitable for complicated projects with many streams of activity, where tasks may take place out of order or in tandem, or where priorities and requirements can change throughout. Waterfall is easy to understand because it follows linear sequencing.
- Critical Path: Project planning based on the time it will take to complete each task, and the "slack time" required between these activities. This includes estimates about what occurs if a task is late or early. This is a fairly straightforward approach, but assumes that people provide reasonable estimates. If the completion of the project is not time-sensitive, this makes sense. The drawback is that people take more time to complete their section than they need if it is allotted to them. This means that projects are unlikely to end early, and may take more time than absolutely necessary.
- Critical Chain: Project planning that looks at time estimates from team members, and then assumes that tasks will not take as long as reported. This is because people either procrastinate or spend time "gold plating" their part of the task, if they are given the extra time. Project plans are created by significantly reducing estimates in order to put pressure on people to deliver their part without spending more time than needed. The extra time is added to the end of the project, in case it is actually required. If the project is time-sensitive, this approach makes the most sense. The

drawback is that it stresses staff, who are pressured to complete activities quicker than initially intended.

- Agile: Agile methodology approaches project management from the perspective of discrete tasks. These tasks are assigned in short bursts, called sprints, which usually last a week or two. At the beginning of each sprint, the group meets to determine which tasks should be completed. At the end of the sprint, the group comes together again to determine what tasks are next. The strength of this approach is that it allows for flexibility, and new tasks can be added even in sprints that occur later on. Furthermore, because each sprint is short, team members are motivated to finish discrete, assigned tasks without wasting time. The goal is not so much to follow a plan, but rather to build collaborative relationships with team members and stakeholders, and to respond to changes as necessary. This is the strength of Agile, as it allows for a process that is flexible and reactive to new requirements. One drawback is the significant time commitment because of the frequent meetings Agile requires. Another drawback is the lack of a more traditional project plan. Team members might find this disorienting, especially in libraries where well-articulated plans are the norm. Scrum is a popular type of Agile framework.
- Kanban: Kanban is less of a project management framework and more of a visualization tool. Projects managed by Kanban center around a central "board" with cards listing tasks that need to be completed. As team members take on tasks, they move the cards from the "to do" column on the board, to the "doing" column, to the "done" column. As bottlenecks occur, processes and workflows are changed to relieve them. This is not a strategy that works well with large projects that have many moving pieces, or for those that require a strong central leader. This approach is focused on helping teams of people organize their own work, rather than being managed from above. With Kanban, existing roles and responsibilities are "respected," allowing for less rigid assignments specific to the project. This means that the role somebody already fills in the organization is also the role they fill on the team. The simplicity of this approach, as well as the flexibility, makes it suitable for any number of smaller projects that might occur in a library.
- Lean: Lean project management focuses on the value to the customer, in this case the library patron or stakeholder. Any activity that doesn't contribute value to the customer is removed from the project plan. The project continues only if there is a "pull," or demand, from the customer, in contrast to many other approaches that are based on a "push" from management. In a library, the purchase of resources through a patron-driven acquisitions model, versus a more traditional librarian-based paradigm, is an example of a "pull," rather than a "push." Lean project management does not work well with projects that are loosely defined. Lean is most commonly used in product manufacturing and supply chain management. One well-known offshoot of Lean is just-in-time inventorying.
- PRINCE2: This is an extremely detailed approach to project management. Roles and responsibilities are defined in minute detail. Projects are divided into clear stages, planned thoroughly at the beginning. Because this approach is formalized and involves a high degree of definition, it is useful for large or complicated projects that require buy-in from lots of different kinds of stakeholders with varying levels of authority. Though this approach is, at times, more flexible than Waterfall, it is not as adaptable as some of the others. Additionally, the attention to detail with this approach makes it time-consuming to implement.

With so many approaches to choose from, picking the right style for the projects is important.

Probably the most noteworthy point to remember when picking a project management approach is that some of these choices require a significant time investment for the planning phase. Others require less of an investment in the planning phase, but may be too flexible for a large project. For many libraries, something as simple as a Kanban board is sufficient for a lot of projects, since it is probably the most versatile and easy to use. That said, a Kanban board isn't enough for complicated projects that include high-ranking officials from across the organization. In this instance, an approach like PRINCE2 often works better, since it defines roles and tasks in great detail. This kind of approach ensures that the roles of people with differing levels of authority are clear from the beginning, hopefully cutting down on the amount of positioning for seniority that might take place. In technical services departments, a lean approach might make the best sense, since their workflows are similar to those in industry.

Another thing to remember is that, while practitioners of each of these choices are sometimes beholden to the style in which they have gained expertise, there are good and bad elements to each. Some projects may require different aspects of varying approaches, combined in a way that makes the most sense to the members of the team. This is heresy to people who are dedicated to Agile or Lean, for instance, but ultimately, the best approach is whatever mix of elements gets the work done as efficiently as possible—that's the whole point.

## The Mythical Man-Month and Late Projects

One final note about projects that run over. In every project manager's life, a little lateness occurs from time to time. In most cases, the project was planned meticulously. The team formed, stormed, and normed. Everything seemed like it was going fine. Then one day it dawns on the project manager that "we're not going to make it." The project is going to be late. Despite the adept use of Scrum, the weekly meetings, and the clearly defined milestones, something has gone terribly wrong. What happens next?

The first thing is not to panic. Figure out what the hard due dates are, the ones that are absolutely essential. Maybe the project is due on November 1, but the office that needs it can hold off until December 2. Maybe one milestone can take longer, as long as four others stay right on track. Every manager experiences late projects on occasion, and as long as the potential for lateness is honestly conveyed to the stakeholders who most need the project, a group can work around this obstacle.

The second thing to do is to figure out why the project is late. There may be a bottleneck somewhere, because the task being held up is required for other things to reach completion. It's possible that a task took longer than expected because of poor time estimations, more complexity, or additional requirements added late in the process. Maybe the resources for the project ran out and the team had to find more funds or manpower. Sometimes projects fall behind because they are too ambitious, and their scope exceeds what is doable for the limited resources or amount of time allotted. The team could be the reason the project has gone off track—if the team, as assembled, doesn't have the right abilities, then the project won't get done. Figure out what the problem is and focus on fixing it—make a plan to unstick bottlenecks, get new staff or reallocate existing staff, and limit the scope and priorities. Team members may also have to work overtime, though there is a limit to how much people are willing or able to do while still performing at a high level and without impacting staff morale.

Remember, though, simply throwing new people at the project won't unstick it. This concept is called Brooks's law: more manpower will only make late projects later, because of the time required to bring new team members on board and to communicate their role on the project (Brooks 1995). It comes from one of the most famous project management books ever written, *The Mythical Man-Month*, by Fredrick Brooks (1995). Every manager should be aware of this book and the impact it has on team-building. In this book, the mythical man-month is not some creature out of a fantasy novel, like a hobbit or a blast-ended screwt. Rather, this is the general principle that a "man-month" as a static measurement of time to finish a project doesn't truly exist (Brooks 1995). More people do not necessarily make a project go faster or run smoother, because workflows don't allow for all tasks to be done in unison, though throwing more people at a late project is often the first impulse of a new manager.

This points to something else that every manager should recognize: the team makes all the difference. A team of twenty student workers might be cheaper and have more hours, but they won't necessarily complete a project faster than two librarians. The student workers have to be trained, scheduled, and guided, not to mention supervised. They probably require a more intense management framework, since they know less about how libraries work. The students are also likely to make more mistakes, which requires the manager to do many more checks and rechecks of their end product. This is all to say that frameworks can only do so much to speed up a project. Having the right team to start with—not more people, necessarily, but the right people—determines how well a project stays on track.

## ⊚ Key Points

- Styles of project management can be very flexible, very rigid, or somewhere in between.
- Each style is useful in different contexts. The one best suited for a project is determined by the context, as well as the manager.
- When a project is late, project managers must identify the reasons for the lateness, and identify the hard due dates that must be met.
- More people are often not the solution for a late project.

## ⊚ References

Allan, Barbara. 2017. *The No-Nonsense Guide to Project Management*. London: Facet Publishing.

Brooks Jr., Frederick. 1995. *The Mythical Man-Month: Essays on Software Engineering*, Anniversary edition. Boston: Addison-Wesley.

Kwak, Young Hoon, John Walewski, Dana Sleeper, and Hessam Sadatsafavi. 2014. "What Can We Learn from the Hoover Dam Project That Influenced Modern Project Management?" *International Journal of Project Management* 32: 256–64. ScienceDirect.

Searcy, Carly Wiggins. 2018. *Project Management in Libraries: On Time, On Budget, On Target*. Chicago: ALA Editions.

# Assessment Basics

THE WORLD IS AWASH IN DATA, and libraries are no exception. In fact, one of the earliest ruminations on the problems of big data came from Fremont Rider, a former director of the Olin Memorial Library at Wesleyan University. Rider published *The Scholar and the Future of the Research Library*, which posited that by 2040, Yale University Libraries would house 200 million books, given that collections were doubling in size every sixteen years (1944). He was a bit off. As of this writing, Yale has only 15 million volumes, with twenty years to go (Sider 2020). Though he was off on the exact number, Rider identified a problem that still plagues libraries today. Too much data is as challenging as too little. His focus on innovations in indexing and cataloging to solve this problem foresaw many of the changes that have revolutionized libraries over the last fifty years, though they preceded the digital revolution by many decades.

Though the data problem that Rider concerned himself with was the ever-expanding production of scientific knowledge, this first lesson is perhaps the most important for the relatively smaller data sets used for library assessment. Too much data buries the most important decision points. This seems to be the primary reason that new managers come to hate assessment, or worse yet, to think that it has little value. So much assessment is obligatory, inundated as libraries are with requirements for the collection of metrics, that the important bits of information that could really drive improvement are buried. The amount of effort needed to gather these mountains of data seem like busywork, and the value might not be readily apparent. In this environment, assessment becomes a four-letter word, and leaders start to agree with the title of one recent article in the *Chronicle of Higher Education*, which proclaimed that "assessment is an enormous waste of time" (Gilbert 2019). Assessment is reduced to compulsory drudgery that doesn't make any real difference.

The reality is that holding assessment in such low regard is a real mistake. Even if a leader never grows to love assessment, its value shouldn't be overlooked. Assessment is the language that leaders of an organization speak, and if the library isn't also talking in these terms, it won't have the real impact it needs to get things done. Furthermore, good data that shows established patterns relevant to the operations of a project, department, or the library as a whole, provide an important window into the reality on the ground. Not to mention that, even when it's most hated, there's no way to get out of doing assessment. Might as well learn how.

## Definitions

Baseline data: Data that reflects the situation before a project or interventions begin. This data will provide a record of how the data change over time.

Benchmarking: The practice of calibrating outcomes against similar data.

COUNTER: The standardized method for recording usage of electronic library resources.

Direct measures: Objective measures that look at proficiencies and outcomes.

Human subjects review: The process of review at universities and other research institutions that ensures researchers treat subjects in an ethical way that doesn't do harm.

Indirect measures: Subjective data that looks at perceptions, beliefs, and attitudes.

Qualitative data: Data that can describe something, but cannot be quantified.

Quantitative data: Data that can be measured, or quantified.

## What Is the Purpose of Assessment?

There are some libraries that perform assessment for one very specific reason: it's required, either by the larger organization or by accreditors. People who complete assessment because they must usually only go far enough to show they've done something or, even better, that they've done something well. There's a place for this kind of assessment, particularly when trying to show impact for things like budget requests, but it's not enough. If this is the beginning and end of an assessment program, the opportunity to make data-driven decisions is missed.

This is to say that assessment should also be done to get information that guides the library in new directions or toward improving existing ones. This category of assessment is more important to the librarian than it is to administrators. The best library leaders can give an accurate, data-driven assessment of what they're doing well and where they're struggling, and they can translate that information into actionable recommendations for what needs to happen next.

In addition to showing what has been done and guiding decisions, there is also assessment for accountability purposes. Sometimes it is tempting to lump together assessment for accountability with assessment that shows what has been accomplished, but it is important to resist this impulse. Assessment for accountability has to be honest and accurate. For instance, if the project involves grant funding, the funding agency likely requires certain assessment data to keep the team accountable. This data must be accurate in order to continue receiving funding from the organization. Accreditation also requires an accurate assessment of activities. In these cases, showing data related to both strengths and weaknesses is imperative—it is better to recognize weaknesses, and to show how they are being mitigated, than to let a grant writer or accreditor discover them on their own. Simply showing what was accomplished—or even better, what was done really well—isn't sufficient because it isn't the goal. The goal is demonstrating where the project has succeeded and where it has failed.

Take from this the fact that, if assessment is done right, an assessment culture is created, one in which data is collected and analyzed for a myriad of reasons. When managing a project, data is key to really understanding what is happening. At the same time, don't collect data just to collect it. Numbers need to be meaningful and purposeful—otherwise, the really important information is buried under an avalanche.

## Basic Principles of Assessment

Goals and milestones were discussed in the chapter about project management frameworks. These goals should be the underlying foundation of any assessment created for a project. There are also chapters about strategic planning later in this book related to larger organizational contexts, but not every project will go through a large-scale strategic planning process. Even without this large-scale process, most projects have a single overarching goal. Start with this goal. What metrics allow a measurement of success for it? For instance, for a project to build an educational resource collection, what does success look like once the collection is created? Who uses it, and what are user expectations for it? How should the resources circulate? Answers to these questions help determine what metrics gauge the overall achievement of the project.

Smaller goals may also be used as guideposts for assessment. Sometimes this is simple. If a project is to catalog a five-hundred-volume donation, and 25 percent must be completed by September 1, how many volumes is that? Some are more complicated. Let's say the project is to start an information literacy program. The goal is to have 25 percent of the student population information literate after the second year. Measuring that might be complicated. A meaningful way to calculate information literacy attainment in the students must be identified. In this case, a rubric could measure the level of literacy, such as the Information Literacy VALUE rubric from the Association of American Colleges and Universities (2009) or the Association of Colleges and Research Libraries rubric based on the ACRL Framework for Information Literacy (2016). If a rubric is chosen, who rates how well students match up to the categories on the rubric? Does this rater use products from coursework or an inventory of some kind? Which students take the inventory if that is the chosen path, and at what point in their degree program? This demonstrates how many decisions need to be made for some types of assessment, and how intricate these can get. This chapter returns to the information literacy example several times, because it is an excellent illustration of a seemingly small task with a substantial degree of complexity.

### Meaningful Assessment

Meaningful assessment, simply put, is assessment that actually measures what it's intended to measure. This is important because far more is learned from a few assessments that provide important, targeted information than from a lot of assessment with data that don't communicate much. There are many new leaders who think they need to collect all of the data they can, all of the time. The reality is that collecting all the data, all the time is exhausting. Again, the real, actionable information gets buried. A smaller number of data points that really get at what a manager wants to know is much more valuable. Let's consider the previous example of the new information literacy program. How could the quality of the new program be evaluated? What is a meaningful evaluation in this case?

To start with, the meaning of "quality" would need to be defined. Does it mean a program in which students achieve certain predetermined learning outcomes? Does it mean a program that students or faculty rate highly on satisfaction surveys? Does it mean a program that leads to students who use better quality sources for their assignments following information literacy instruction? If student achievement of certain learning outcomes needs to be measured, a student satisfaction survey probably isn't meaningful. If the degree to which students perform on their assignments after information literacy instruction is what is required, a pre-test and post-test that actually look at how they use research in writing assignments is valuable. This is to say that the definition of quality frames how a meaningful assessment is defined.

Meaningful also means figuring out which of these assessments is most important to showing achievement, fulfilling accountability requirements, and identifying weaknesses and strengths, relative to the amount of work needed to collect each type of data. While some data might be useful, collecting the data might take so much time that the value is negated. In this case, a citation study of student data would take a lot of time and effort, possibly more than what would be gained if done on a large scale. The assessment of learning outcomes through a testing measure and a rubric would probably be more feasible on a routine basis, but would still require a non-negligible amount of effort. The easiest option is the satisfaction survey, but such surveys are indirect assessments, and probably give the least amount of hard, actionable data relevant to the project. As a result, the assessment of learning outcome achievement is probably the best option for meaningful data when comparing effort to benefit, especially since it also happens to line up with the way other academic departments talk about their assessment at universities. This helps administrators outside of the library understand the data, since it is common across academia.

Collecting all three types of data on a routine basis probably isn't desirable, because that would be data overkill. Picking the most meaningful data points is key, or those that gauge quality relevant to the operant definition of quality. Sometimes there is a tendency to default to a satisfaction survey, even in those cases where a satisfaction survey won't give direct evidence of successes and weaknesses. Another example of this mismatch in measure might be an assessment of circulation, where the quality of customer service needs to be quantified. Looking at the increases and decreases in checkouts won't really give that information, but a satisfaction survey probably would.

## Quantitative and Qualitative Data

Another question when doing assessment is whether quantitative data or qualitative data, or both, should be collected. Quantitative data is data that can be measured. Qualitative data is data that describes something, but cannot be quantified. The data gathered from multiple-choice surveys is likely quantitative—that is, a certain percentage of people chose a, b, c, or d. The data gathered from an open-ended question, such as one asking for further comments or concerns, is qualitative. Both of these types of data are valuable when doing assessment, and both should be gathered when possible.

Quantitative data is useful when objective information is needed, or when patterns across data are important, and might not be evident if looking at singular responses from individual participants. Much of the data that library leaders analyze is quantitative and include circulation and usage statistics, financial information, survey data, and collection analyses. As a result, having a good understanding of statistics is important. There are many books out there that can help people brush up on statistics, including the wildly popular *Statistics for People Who (Think They) Hate Statistics* by Neil Salkind and Bruce Frey (2019). If analyzing quantitative data is a real struggle, auditing a statistics class to get a handle on the topic might be in order.

Qualitative data tends to be more nuanced, providing contextual information from individual participants. This is especially useful when individualized feedback might contribute to understanding an issue more fully. It also allows participants to direct attention to the things they are most concerned with, which may not be readily apparent to the survey designer. For instance, an open-ended question on a satisfaction survey allows patrons to mention things that they find problematic about the library, which a director might not otherwise hear about, such as a noise problem in a quiet area or a need for pencils and staplers on a floor where they aren't currently stocked. The librarians might not know they need to ask about these issues, but an open-ended question allows users to draw attention to them.

Though quantitative data tends to be more plentiful, don't discount the importance of qualitative data. Things come out in qualitative data that are not predictable. For instance, an open-ended question might garner multiple complaints about having no printer on the second floor of the library. Though in hindsight, the need for the printer might be obvious, library staff often won't see it until it jumps out in multiple responses. This is why it is so important to provide opportunities for patrons to bring up whatever issues they want on surveys—the things they are concerned about might not be the things that the library staff are concerned about.

## Direct and Indirect Data

Having both direct and indirect sources of data is also important when assessing a project. Direct measures are objective measures and are concerned with proficiencies, outcomes, and other hard data. These are important because they show, objectively, how the library is performing in certain respects. Direct measures for a library might include a skills test that looks at what a student can do following a library instruction session, a list of circulation statistics by collection, or an inventory of resources that show how many items are on the shelves, and whether those items are in the right place.

Indirect data is subjective data that looks at perceptions, beliefs, and attitudes. Indirect data is important because it shows how stakeholders view what has been accomplished. This kind of data illustrates whether the library's work is meaningful to the people who most depend on it. If the library is accomplishing a lot objectively, but receiving poor marks on subjective measures like user satisfaction, it could be that the library staff missed something that is going wrong, or maybe staff members aren't communicating the library's story well to stakeholders. These subjective measures might include user satisfaction surveys and other feedback from stakeholders.

## Benchmarking and Baseline Data

Benchmarking is the practice of calibrating expectations for outcomes against other, similar data from equivalent organizations or groups. To benchmark data, library staff must identify data sources that are similar enough to compare. Baseline data can also be gathered, and then changes in the data can be tracked over time. Comparable data might be available from lots of different sources, including state and national surveys like the ACRL Trends survey (2020), or library tools, like OCLC's collection comparison tools (2018). Most of these data sets allow filtering of results until comparable data is identified that roughly approximates an institution. New leaders should find these sources and get to know them well. Being able to navigate benchmarking data is incredibly handy, because it provides the ability to show stakeholders and the administration that the project, department, or library is on target. Deficiencies are also demonstrable with benchmarking data, such as numbers of librarians or the size of collections.

When benchmarking, it's a good idea to create a list of peer and aspirational institutions—other libraries like the one being measured for peer institutions, or those that are what a library someday wishes to be for aspirational institutions. These are the libraries that a leader will go to first when comparing data. For projects, this might involve finding similar ventures at other, analogous institutions. Either way, comparing what the library is doing to what other people at similar organizations are doing is a good way to show whether realistic objectives are being met.

In addition to benchmarking, baseline data is also useful. This is data that reflects the situation before the project or intervention begins. This data helps demonstrate how the situation changes over time, and the difference that the project or intervention has made. Baseline data can include many things, including pre-tests.

## Designing Data Collection

The topic of research design is a big one, and there are many, many excellent books written about it, including *Research Design: Qualitative, Quantitative, and Mixed Methods Approaches* by John W. Creswell and J. David Creswell (2018). While this section can provide an overview, managers would do well to dive into the topic on their own, and to learn as much as possible.

When designing data collection, the first decision to make is how the data will be used once it's collected, and most importantly, whether the data is going to be published or reviewed internally. If the data will be published, more stringent data collection practices are required. In many cases, human subject review is also needed if people are involved in the research. Human subject review and approval is the process of review at universities and other research institutions that ensures researchers are treating subjects in an ethical way, and aren't harming them. If data won't be published, the guidelines are less stringent, but for those who are faculty, treating all assessment as though it might lead to publication is usually a productive approach. It is unfortunate to reach the end of a survey or other research project and realize that the findings can't be published because the project never underwent human subject review.

Though library assessment can take many forms, most managers spend a lot of their time designing surveys because these are often the easiest way to solicit user feedback in a customer-focused environment. All library leaders should have at least one go-to survey design volume on the bookshelf to ensure they are following best practices. Survey design can be tricky, and requires a degree of skill that is difficult for a novice to attain. That said, here is a very rough list of principles related to survey design to help managers get started:

- Leading questions: Questions should not lead participants to answer in a certain way. For instance, consider the question "How would you rate the service you received?" versus "How good was the service you received?" The phrasing of the former is better because it doesn't prime respondents to answer that their service experience was good. Because people are inclined to try to answer the way a surveyor wants, the latter is more leading than the former. The latter is also biased, by suggesting that the library service was good, even if it wasn't.
- Survey length: Keep surveys short and focused. Sometimes, when designing a survey, everyone involved wants a question. Resist this urge. Focus surveys on the information needed to best understand the principal question.
- Expectations: Be transparent with respondents. Tell them how many questions are on the survey, how long it will take, and how the data will be used. Give clear instructions about how to take the survey. Let people know if there are any incentives—snacks and candy are always popular!
- Sections: Break the survey up into sections with a few questions in each section. This makes survey takers feel like they are progressing more quickly, and also helps organize the flow. The most important section of questions should go first, so that people who stop taking it partway through still provide essential data. Demographic data, for instance, might come at the end if it is least important.
- Clear wording: Use plain language. Surveys should be easy to understand and answer. Don't use lots of specialized terms.
- Demographic questions: Ask demographic questions, but only those demographic questions that are actually meaningful. For instance, on a survey about patterns of library use, gender demographics might not be especially helpful, but academic major would be. Demographic data is powerful because it can allow more complicated and interesting analyses, but it can also add a lot of length to a survey.
- Anonymity: Take steps to ensure the anonymity of respondents, and let them know about these steps. People answer more honestly when they know they are anonymous.
- Sample size: Know how many people are needed for the sample and focus on getting a good representative sample, rather than just a large number of respondents. Sometimes offering a better prize to a selected, statistically significant group of participants, such as a specially branded t-shirt or mug, can garner good results.

This is just a short list of best practices for survey design. Again, anyone doing surveys should really read a book about the topic, as surveys require a degree of skill to do well. Also, remember that there are predesigned surveys for big topics like library satisfaction and quality, such as LibQual+ (Association of Research Libraries n.d.), and participating in one of these can be really useful for libraries. Often, participants get detailed data about the responses, benchmarked against other, similar libraries. The drawback of these large-scale surveys is that they cost quite a bit of money.

Keep in mind that designing research, and especially data-gathering methods, is important for benchmarking and collecting baseline data. When data is being benchmarked against an existing data set, collection should take place in a way as similar as possible to the original data. For data that will be compared to baseline data, it should be collected in the same way every year. Most national- and state-level surveys have handbooks that describe how data is collected and for what periods of time. One of the most important steps for any library in this regard is deciding what the annual statistical reporting period is. For instance, some libraries use academic year, especially if this also happens to be the institution's fiscal year. By setting this as the annual reporting period, almost all of the data reported runs according to this schedule. This makes data collection and comparison much easier over a period of time, and across data sets.

Really think about the way data is collected, and even audit data collection from time to time to make sure mistakes aren't being made. Mistakes happen easily, even when collecting simple data. For instance, the library's electronic periodical holdings are probably run every year. The platforms used to run this data add new features over time, and might add novel ways to limit things like duplicate titles. Reviewing how data is run on an annual basis ensures that better methods of running data are apparent if they are made available. Another example is the way libraries run ebook usage using COUNTER, the standardized method for recording usage of electronic library resources. There's more than one way of running these reports, and the approach used can greatly change the numbers that are retrieved. Librarians have to think about which version of the data makes the most sense in each context. Moreover, grant organizations, as well as national and state surveys, have specific ways they want data recorded, so it's important to review their data manuals and requirements before information is collected in order to ensure that it is done right. Bad data, when discovered, can result in hours of extra work!

One simple way to audit data is to look at the numbers run in the past for the same statistical point. If the data is significantly more or less than what was previously recorded, and there is no clear explanation for why, then something might be wrong. Another way to ensure accurate data is to regularly check formulas in spreadsheets to make sure they are all correct.

## Reporting

How and when data is reported is determined by multiple factors. For projects that are grant funded, reporting is likely to be regularized, and the requirements come from the granting organization. Most such organizations have formal systems for submitting data, and many also have their own surveys and other data collection measures. Annual data that's collected by the library is probably submitted to state agencies, or national surveys such as ACRL Library Trends (ACRL 2020) or IPEDs data collection (National Center for Education Statistics 2020). Institutions likely also have some institutional effectiveness requirements that require data as well.

For data collected to inform the library administration of accomplishments, consider the most impactful way to report the information. Some of this can be effective marketing for the institution if it's put on a website in a way that's accessible and targeted. Some of it might not need to be written up in anything more formal than an email. Don't overdo it! This is one of the biggest mistakes young library directors make—too much formal reporting of data. Data should be recorded in a meaningful way, where it can be accessed later as needed, and interpreted against past years. This doesn't require formal reports for every kind of assessment. Sometimes, when everything is reported in a formal context, the most important data—the data people should notice—gets lost in the mix. Be selective and curate information in meaningful ways for different audiences. Shape the narrative!

Of course, curating data doesn't mean editing out the bad points. To circle back to meaningful data collection, report the things that are stellar per the data, but also the places where the library could do a better job. Highlighting these data points to the administration can help make a case for more resources, or different resources. Editing out the bad points doesn't always help, because data that shows weaknesses makes a concrete argument for places where the administration can help the library grow.

However data is reported, remember that libraries have been organizing big data since the beginning. Indexing and cataloging the exponential growth of scientific knowledge is what libraries do, and as a result, librarians are very good at presenting data. There's been a lot of talk recently about how libraries can get buy-in from skeptical stakeholders who don't see their value. One way might be to play on the strengths of many librarians—this ability to organize data meaningfully. Really, that is all assessment comes down to—collecting and presenting information that shows something meaningful to an audience, even if the audience is just the rest of the library staff.

## Key Points

- Assessment should be built from goals and measures of how well they are met.
- Assessment should be meaningful and impactful.
- Quantitative and qualitative data, as well as direct and indirect data, are all important to ensure meaningful assessment that looks at an issue in a variety of ways.
- Benchmarking data and creating baseline data sets provide ways to measure the data collected against other, similar metrics.

## References

Association of American Colleges and Universities. 2009. "Information Literacy VALUE Rubric." https://www.aacu.org/value/rubrics/information-literacy.

Association of College and Research Libraries. 2016. "Framework for Information Literacy for Higher Education." January 11. http://www.ala.org/acrl/standards/ilframework.

———. 2020. "ACRL 2019–20 Academic Library Trends and Statistics Survey." https://acrl .countingopinions.com/.

Association of Research Libraries. n.d. "About LibQual+." Accessed November 21, 2020. https:// www.libqual.org/about/about_lq.

Creswell, John W., and J. David Creswell. 2018. *Research Design: Qualitative, Quantitative, and Mixed Methods Approaches*. Fifth Edition. Los Angeles: Sage Publications.

Gilbert, Erik. 2019. "Assessment Is an Enormous Waste of Time." *Chronicle of Higher Education*, March 20. https://www.chronicle.com/article/assessment-is-an-enormous-waste-of-time /#:~:text=The%20fundamental%20claim%20of%20the,courses%2C%20curricula%2C%20 and%20colleges.

National Center for Education Statistics. 2020. "IPEDS Data Collection System." https://surveys .nces.ed.gov/IPEDS/.

OCLC. 2018. "Assessment Tools." https://help.oclc.org/Librarian_Toolbox/OCLC_Usage _Statistics/140Assessment_Tools?sl=en.

Rider, Fremont. 1944. *The Scholar and the Future of the Research Library: A Problem and Its Solution*. New York: Hadham Press.

Salkind, Neil J., and Bruce B. Frey. 2019. *Statistics for People Who (Think They) Hate Statistics*. Seventh Edition. Los Angeles: Sage Publications.

Sider, Laura. 2020. "How Many Books Are at Yale University Library?" Ask Yale Library, April 7. https://ask.library.yale.edu/faq/175105#:~:text=Our%20collection%20at%20Yale%20Univer sity,printed%20books%20to%20electronic%20databases.

# CHAPTER 6

# Developing Professionally through Project Management

THINK OF THIS FIRST PART OF THE BOOK AS A GUIDE to the way librarians with little or no management experience might describe their involvement leading projects in order to land that first middle management job in a library. The skills and concepts covered herein are some of the most essential in order to be successful, at least in the interview. Though that first management job often can seem impossible to secure without actual administrative experience, it will be a lot simpler approached from this perspective.

When applying to a middle management role, remember that these positions often lead self-sustaining units in the library. These units function independently, and the manager is expected to keep the wheels on, as it were, without a lot of hand-holding. A middle manager who can't keep a unit productive is a headache for the director. In interviews, successful candidates convince the director that their past experience has prepared them to jump into the role, without a lot of intervention.

Candidates for this kind of position might not have a lot of experience with budgeting, human resources (HR) policy, or compliance, but the director probably won't expect these kinds of competencies unless the position is at a particularly large or important library, or is directly related to those hard skills. What the hiring manager does expect for middle management positions is someone who understands the soft skills. Oftentimes, this corresponds to preferences for candidates who have managed others or who are proficient with certain types of management styles. Past involvement with project management can satisfy this preference, provided it is described appropriately during the interview.

For instance, explaining a preferred leadership style, developed while managing a project, can be an excellent way to demonstrate the type of leader a candidate will be if hired by an institution. Experiences navigating the development stages of a group, and mediating between member personalities, also helps potential employers see how a librarian leads when others report to them. An anecdote about the way a reluctant team member was motivated to get their work done, or how a conflict was resolved during a group project, can go a long way toward convincing a hiring manager that a librarian has the skills to supervise. After all, the leadership skills gained from project management directly correlate to what managers do every day.

While soft skills predominate, there are some hard skills that may be learned from project management. Assessment is one such hard skill. In fact, it is one of the most important skills to demonstrate when seeking a move into library management. Assessment might seem mystifying, but it is also essential to many of the daily tasks of a manager: allocating resources, making decisions, and identifying weaknesses. For this reason, potential managers who understand assessment are an asset to any future employer. Most library directors recognize this. The reality is that a middle manager with assessment experience is starting two steps ahead of one without.

Demonstrating an understanding of library assessment is also a way to telegraph that a potential manager can think in the way required for management. Someone who can think through assessment, and make decisions based on the data, is someone who can cut a budget when needed and make tough, unpopular decisions. This is also someone who is likely able to understand compliance issues. Sometimes people go into management but aren't ready to make the kinds of real-world decisions that managers face every day. Showing an ability use data in these situations demonstrates the right perspective for such dilemmas from an institutional standpoint.

Keep in mind that the management of smaller projects, whether formal or informal, is often the precursor to a more permanent management role at your current institution. Approach these opportunities with intentionality. Directors often hand out projects to prepare strong employees to move up in the organization. They "try out" someone's leadership skills before such an opportunity opens up. Make the most of the tryout! Everyone has to start somewhere. Just because these types of projects don't provide permanent employees or job changes, doesn't mean that they can't have a real impact on the trajectory of a career.

In order to make the most of these opportunities, be sure to document management experiences and roles as best as you can. Write down different activities, problems the project faced, and how they were resolved. Be able to identify an ideal leadership style and discuss how team dynamics can impact performance. Have a plan for how to motivate reluctant employees, and consider how to discuss these experiences in a way that shows concrete competencies, not just a textbook understanding. Remember to mirror back the language of the hiring committee when talking about management experience, and also learn how to talk with confidence about past leadership. Imposter syndrome, or the feeling that one is unqualified for a position that is actually a good match, is something every leader has to work through at some point. Sometimes, projecting confidence, even if it's a little insincere, can help build true self-assurance when it matters. As a former colleague used to say, "fake it until you make it."

# Part II

# MIDDLE MANAGEMENT

# CHAPTER 7

# The Role of the Middle Manager

*Sometimes you have to take a break from being the kind of boss that's always trying to teach people things. Sometimes you just have to be the boss of dancing.*

—MICHAEL SCOTT (2006)

AIRING FOR NINE SEASONS IN THE UNITED STATES, *The Office* is a wildly popular workplace sitcom. Set at Dunder Mifflin, a struggling paper company, and featuring Michael Scott, the quintessential middle manager played by Steve Carrell, the sitcom focuses on the relationships that develop between employees. Though Scott sometimes seems inept, many episodes of *The Office* actually depict the role of a middle manager pretty accurately. Scott struggles with wanting to be a colleague and a mentor, and he muddies both roles by being too chummy, until the situation inevitably turns on him and he has to be the boss again. He frequently has to implement policies from corporate that he doesn't agree with or like, and he spends an inordinate amount of time dealing with personnel issues, to the point where he hates his HR manager, Toby Flenderson. Scott was hired for the job because he was a truly great salesman, and he obviously loves sales, but he now spends his time handling situations for which he seems unprepared. Whatever one's expectation of middle management might be, Michael Scott is closer to the reality than is likely comfortable. That said, Scott actually is effective, in his own inimitable way, and the people who work for him admire him a great deal. The fact that he genuinely cares about them shines through, even when his antics and mistakes are at their worst.

While the first experience with sustained leadership that most librarians get is at the level of middle manager, the popularity of *The Office* ensures that most people are familiar with Michael Scott, the quintessential middle manager, long before they actually get the job. Throughout this chapter, keep him in mind. Though he's not an example of a perfect mid-level manager, he is an example of a human one. Like Scott, middle managers in libraries are at the center of things, squeezed between the director and everyone else, often tasked with carrying out the administration's vision and policies while also dealing with complaints from staff when these directives are unpopular. Being in such a liminal position is a real challenge, often described as feeling sandwiched between the edicts of those above and the needs of those below. Middle managers have to navigate the space between these countervailing forces.

In addition to being a liminal role, middle management in libraries can also feel like shooting down a hill in a soapbox cart. At this level things happen awfully fast, sometimes too fast to keep up. Luckily, though this is stressful, it isn't the grand prix and there are still bales of hay around the perimeter to soften the blow if the cart goes careening off the track. This is to say that middle managers do a lot at the library, picking up one task after another, and sometimes taking on responsibility for things with which they have no experience. When something goes truly wrong, the library executive is there to help. This is like providing training wheels to new managers, to ensure that mistakes can be righted.

This sensation of a downhill slalom is exacerbated by the fact that middle managers are usually performing aspects of the job they previously held as a reference librarian, cataloger, or e-resources librarian, but with a host of added duties. The first, and most time-consuming, of these are supervisory responsibilities. Obviously, learning how to supervise others, both from a mentoring perspective and a human resource perspective, is a huge requirement for any future director. People who have never supervised don't realize the time commitment required. Working with employees takes up a lot of time and can be emotionally draining because it requires dealing with complicated situations. Many who have these supervisory responsibilities find that employees take up far more time than any other part of their job. Supervising others is also difficult to do well. There's a tightrope between overmanaging, by either micromanaging or mentoring in a way that's overly familiar, and undermanaging, by failing to provide direction or professional guidance. Managers on both ends of the spectrum tend to create problems for directors, and as a middle manager, one of the main goals is to avoid such problems. A pattern of problems usually occurs because the department needs constant small interventions for small issues, or because big problems aren't addressed until they are so significant, the director has to step in.

For middle managers, avoiding this pattern of problems means knowing how to ensure the department stands on its own two feet on the one hand, and knowing when problems need to be brought to the director on the other. This is to say that middle management develops a leader's sense of authority, as well as the limitations of that authority. While the focus of many leadership books is having a sense of one's own power, and the confidence to make decisions and take charge, knowing the limitations of a role is also hugely important. Middle managers who make decisions above their pay grade quickly learn that they are a liability to the director. Knowing the limits of one's mandate, and being able to exercise restraint, develops into a sense of what is and isn't allowed legally, ethically, and professionally. This sense keeps directors from making some very bad decisions, even when they seem like the right ones, and even when the training wheels are off. At the same time, middle managers who bring absolutely every decision to the director won't advance much further in their career, because no one learns to trust their judgement. Directors have to be the singular specialist on library management in their organization. Filling this kind of role takes confidence and determination. It also takes earned trust from those higher up.

This dance between the two impulses is a key way that middle managers learn about leadership, and prepare to advance to executive management. Cultivating that sense of when things should be escalated to higher levels, and when they should be handled and reported—or even not reported—is absolutely essential for directors, and it isn't as easy as it may seem. One key factor is having a director who trusts the middle managers enough to let them make mistakes, and to correct them when they've made those mistakes. Remember, part of the job is to make life easier for the director, and to realize their vision for the library. Trust is essential.

Another important factor for middle managers is the opportunity to allocate resources, participate in strategic planning, and impact the wider organization through interdepartmental projects. These opportunities are not always offered to early-career librarians, but once this level is reached, they become more available. The director often has middle managers serve on committees representing the library. Take these opportunities seriously, as they represent a big part of the director's day-to-day role. These assignments may sometimes feel like busywork, but leaders recommend them to middle managers who show promise for future positions in the organization.

The opportunity to be involved in budgeting and strategic planning decisions is especially important, because these activities comprise the biggest part of a library executive's job, barring perhaps managing people. These are also areas where most librarians have no prior experience, and they are almost always central to interviews for administrative positions. Doing either of these tasks well takes time, which is compounded by the fact that these responsibilities are not interesting to some new supervisors. For a librarian coming from a role of reference librarian, where working with people is the best part of the day, dealing with numbers for hours might not be rewarding, especially the reduction of people to numbers in the form of salaries and performance metrics. While catalogers or metadata librarians might be a little more acclimated to looking at data, the calming, almost meditative, rhythm of library records is not present with budgeting or assessment. These tasks are stressful, frustrating, and rife with uncertainty. This points to one difficult, and ironic, part of becoming a middle manager: at this level, people start to move away from the aspects of the job that they probably enjoyed and did so well that it got them promoted in the first place. The very thing that makes a librarian good enough to become a supervisor is the thing that most librarians lose as they move up into administration. Just as Michael Scott was a great salesman, most managers were once great at another job—so great, they were asked to lead people at the very same thing. For this reason, budgeting and strategic planning at the level of middle management is a warning as much as an opportunity, because it represents the certainty that management is a move toward these other duties and away from one's previous career.

Beyond the more basic need to learn how to manage a budget and perform assessment, understanding the budget and how it is shaped by competing strategic goals helps to move middle managers into a more administrative frame of mind. This means understanding why fluctuations in the funding occur, and how competing goals cause these fluctuations. Sometimes a manager's department has to take a cut because there are bigger needs elsewhere in the library or across the institution. In the first chapter of this book, the joke was about resurfacing the lazy river, but budget exigencies are not often that frivolous. Sometimes funding is cut from the library to add faculty lines in an academic department that is rapidly increasing enrollment. This need is important to the entire institution, dependent as it is on students to fund any number of priorities, including the library. While librarians without this administrative perspective might have a hard time understanding why those faculty lines are more important than the book budget, a librarian with the administrative view understands how funding is an ecosystem, and sometimes taking a cut this year leads to a more sustained increase in student fees later, though it could also be a permanent cut for the good of the institution. Being able to demonstrate an understanding of this broader ecosystem is key to interviews for executive jobs, because provosts and city managers want to know that a director has the more encompassing understanding of finances, not simply the one from inside the four walls of the library.

In addition to these other new duties, middle managers are often responsible for the activities of multiple different areas in the library. Many people at this level supervise related functions like cataloging and acquisitions, or circulation and reference. As a result, these managers can't be single-subject specialists. They have to know something about everything they supervise, at least enough to make informed decisions and set goals. This, too, is a pivotal skill for those who are middle managers, and even more so for those who want to become a director, because library executives represent the entire library, not just an area of specialty. Directors have to make decisions about the library as a whole, in consultation with middle managers. A director who has never cataloged a single book must still understand why cataloging is important, and make decisions about it. Directors also need to maintain balance between areas of the library they know a lot about, and those with which they are less familiar. Middle managers over more than one area have the opportunity to learn how to balance these competing forces.

Finally, to become a director, a librarian must think of himself or herself as a leader. The reality is that leaders have to make unpopular decisions that impact people in unfortunate ways. While they must always be collegial, they also need to remember that playing favorites can lead to uncomfortable or difficult situations. Middle management is an excellent way to learn how to separate being a colleague from being a friend.

With all of these new duties, many people choose never to move beyond middle management. As those new to these positions quickly learn, moving into executive leadership often results in an end to one's old, specialty-based career and the beginning of a new career in administration. There are a lot of people who don't want to leave their practitioner status behind completely. So too, there are plenty of people that want to spend their time thinking and caring about the library, and not the complicated ecosystem that makes up the organization as a whole, whether it's a university or a city. Still others find budgeting, supervising, or strategic planning onerous and stressful. All this is to say that these positions are best approached as opportunities in their own right. A transfer into middle management is a real career move that doesn't have to lead to anything else. Don't overthink it—get the position, and then decide what happens next.

Whatever the next step is, the most important thing to remember is that people respond to authenticity and genuine concern, even when a new manager makes some mistakes. As long as the intentions are true, most people forgive these mistakes. This human approach also allows managers to avoid being too solitary. Supervisors might not be buddies with their employees, but they are mentors, and that is a kind of relationship that can be just as strong. Remember, sometimes it's OK to be the boss of dancing, because celebration is vital to any team. After all, even Michael Scott, with all his foibles, was a pretty good manager.

# References

*The Office*. 2006. "Booze Cruise." Netflix video. 21:02, January 5. https://www.netflix.com/title/70136120.

# Mentoring and Managing Employees

MOST LIBRARIANS FIRST SUPERVISE EMPLOYEES either in library school or pretty quickly after graduation. An undergraduate student worker is assigned to the circulation desk or in the book processing area, and the librarian or library student is expected to keep that undergraduate on track and motivated. There's a lot to learn from this first experience, but many people fall into the trap of thinking that it represents the biggest part of management. In reality, every new employee is a new management experience. Paraprofessionals have different needs than student workers, and so on. Tailoring interactions to the employee is important, because not every staff member needs the same thing, but they all need something. New managers don't always understand this immediately, nor the importance of growing people professionally, even student workers. No matter who the employee is, the best bosses are mentors—the ones who nurture people from one stage of their career into the next.

## Definitions

Mentor: A more experienced colleague who provides professional guidance.

Student involvement theory: A theory of student engagement positing that student success at an institution of higher education is correlated to their involvement with the institution.

In 1968, an MCA/Universal film executive named Sidney Sheinberg saw an amateur short film named *Amblin'* by an up-and-coming young director (Brustein 2018). Based on the quality of that film, the executive offered the director a seven-year contract, noting that he would stick with the young filmmaker in failure, not just success. The executive went on to serve as a mentor to that director throughout his career and, eventually, Steven Spielberg became one of the most celebrated filmmakers of the last fifty years (Brustein 2018). In turn, Spielberg went on to mentor others, like J. J. Abrams and Matt Reeves, giving back to his profession by offering the same opportunities he received (Lewis and Anderman 2016). Per Spielberg, standing by someone in failure, not just success, became "like an anthem" throughout his career, representing the best professional relationships possible (Gallo 2017).

Though Spielberg's talent was obvious, even at a young age, another takeaway from this story is that the right mentor can make the difference. Nurturing and focusing the talents and interests of young people is one of the most important roles of a professional. This is the way that librarians shape what the field becomes, and ensure that there is a new generation prepared to carry on the good work of libraries. Finding talented new librarians, and giving them the opportunities they need to make an impact in their own way, is vital. Not every relationship with an employee develops into mentorship, but those that do are often the most important to both the supervisor and the supervisee. The best bosses, the ones that people remember their whole career, teach them about the profession and help them navigate it when they are growing into the librarian they will become. This entails helping people find their own way, not insisting that they follow the mentor's lead. Sometimes the mentee ends up in a wholly different line of work, having moved into the publishing industry or another area of the university, but that is why the mentoring relationship is so special: it is always fragile, built to hoist someone up until they've outgrown what the mentor can provide, and then it ends, with both people better for it. True mentors give people the tools to succeed, and let them do it on their own.

Remember that mentorship isn't only about the employee. In some respects, management can be quite lonely, but the opportunity to mentor is a real bright spot. Throughout the next chapters of this book, the theme of having to pull away from buddy relationships with other people in the department after moving to management returns again and again, but the opportunity to mentor is what is gained from this trade-off. Acting as someone's mentor is not the same as being their buddy, of course, but it is uniquely satisfying and rewarding in a way that other work friendships are not. This is particularly true for librarians who enjoy working with students through instruction or on the reference desk. As a librarian moves into a director position, the same skills that made them good at student interactions also help effectively guide early-career librarians, student workers, and paraprofessionals.

For managers who have worked in the field for a while, mentoring is also an opportunity to learn about new things, and to see the profession with fresh eyes again. Mentors learn so much from the interests and thoughts of those who are new to the profession that this relationship can be a real driver of innovation. The important thing is to remain enthusiastic and open to change, nurturing the novel ideas that might shape the future of the field. Though much of this chapter is about different management techniques, it all ultimately comes back to mentorship, and advancing librarianship through new practitioners, whatever their ultimate professional destination might be.

# ⊚ Managing Student Workers

The first time a librarian supervises student workers, it is so easy to think of them as just entry-level paraprofessionals with course schedules. They come in and work the circulation desk, shift books, or shelve. They are there for work-study funds, or an hourly wage, and that's about it. This interpretation of the role of student workers doesn't really get at the heart of what they need. Student workers are entirely different from paraprofessionals or librarians, and the structure of their experience should reflect this. They are there to get more than wages. They need valuable work experience that can help improve their connection to campus and ultimately, their success in an academic program. As Michelle Reale says in *Mentoring and Managing Students in the Academic Library*, student workers should be trained "as young adults who will be entering and facing the actual work world" (Reale 2013).

The work of George Kuh, one of the most important theorists studying student engagement in higher education, is pivotal to understanding the significance of student worker positions. Kuh's "involvement theory" posits that "the more time and energy students expend on educationally purposeful activities, the more they benefit" (1995, 125). Kuh and his colleagues used this theory to develop a list of high impact practices that engage students and improve persistence in college (2008). These practices include experiences that allow students to apply what they learn to the real world, including through campus jobs. Every director at a university, and even directors at other kinds of libraries, must be familiar with Kuh's work, because it should guide the way student workers are managed.

In general, there are two kinds of student workers: those who plan to go to library school and become librarians, and those who are simply in the library due to a work-study program or to defray the cost of attendance. Though they are similar, the goal should be to give both types of students meaningful experiences that allow them to use what they are learning and give them valuable skills for when they graduate. Another reason to keep students meaningfully engaged is that they tend to perform better when they are really interested in the work they are doing, because they see its value. Most people who manage student workers have experienced the students who are unreliable, play games on their phone all day, or do homework rather than processing books. Engaged students are much less likely to fall into this category.

Unless one works in a library that is attached to a library science program, most students are simply there to do a part-time job, make some extra money, or fulfill their work-study requirements. Sometimes these students are pursuing degrees in English, accounting, art history, or a myriad of other topics that don't directly correlate with the work they're doing at the library. That doesn't mean that their campus job can't help them reach their professional goals.

When hiring students to work in the library, one of the interview questions should be about their ultimate professional aims. Do they want to go into a customer service–oriented role, become an accountant, or work as a teacher? Try to fit them into a position in the library that might give them related or complementary experiences. For instance, a student who is pursuing a degree in computer science might work in technical services with a librarian who is managing the website, using metadata, or doing digitization work. An accounting or business student may benefit by helping in acquisitions, where a lot of purchasing happens. Business students might also take to circulation, since so much at that desk is focused on frontline customer service. Regardless of where students are hired to work, have a clear idea of the skills they should develop in that position, and how these skills transfer to their post-college life.

Once a student is hired, it's not enough to simply give tasks and expect completion. Structure training to focus on the skills identified when students were hired. Observe them at work on a regular basis, and provide input to help hone these abilities. Check in with them regularly and see what they are learning. Ask them if they are surprised by anything. What do they find challenging? How are things working out? Having student workers keep a journal that documents their experiences allows them to reflect on and grow from what they are doing on the job, and also track their activities so they can use these details to write cover letters when they start job hunting. Even something as simple as shelving can turn into a growth experience. After shelving books, student workers can come up with some ideas about how to better teach fellow undergraduates to find items, based on their difficulties. The point is that everything they do needs to have a purpose, and should contribute to their professional development.

The same is true for library students, but to a more significant degree. Most professional librarians have a good idea of the kinds of competencies that future library employers appreciate, and providing potential librarians with that experience is vital. Give undergraduate students who are planning to go to library school challenging tasks that might set them apart when they apply. This can help those students get into the program they want, and to get scholarships. Experiences using metadata to create artifacts in a digital library, for instance, are rare and impressive, and this type of task is easy enough with strong training. For students who want to go into public services, structured and supervised opportunities to teach peers about research, through an information literacy program, for example, can be extraordinarily important. Though obviously at this level the students may not be ready to man the reference desk on their own, that doesn't mean they can't have some experience teaching others about research with direct supervision, as well as guidance about privacy and ethics.

For graduate library information science (LIS) students, opportunities to work on the desk are even more important. Interns from library science programs should always have a tour on the reference desk if they don't have that experience already, even if they are primarily focused on another area of the library. Most librarians, even those in technical services, should be able to work reference. Having this experience before graduation from a LIS program is exceptionally important. Interns should also be given a chance to practice collection development since, again, almost all librarians have that as a duty at some point in their career. LIS students can also be trained to do copy cataloging or create metadata schema. For LIS interns who are interested in e-resources, training and experience with a link resolver, the administrative side of a discovery service, or vendor interactions are opportunities that they can't get anywhere else. Though the managing librarian must use discretion about the amount of supervision required for different students across different duties, giving LIS students the ability to function as professionals (though sometimes with training wheels) is huge.

Finally, keep in mind that no matter how well a library engages students, there are inevitably student workers who, for one reason or another, have problems that get in the way of success. They are routinely late, they are not skilled in communicating with customers, or they don't understand professional behavior. These students are challenging, but they provide an excellent opportunity to act as a kind of mentor. Again, remember, they are here to learn. The librarian must set expectations for them and teach them what it means to have a job. They may never have had one before, and it's so much better that they learn now, before the stakes become much higher after graduation. If worse comes to worst, and a student worker needs to be fired, better they learn the lesson now than later. In everything, remember that this experience must teach them how to be an employee, and when they get away with unprofessional behavior, it doesn't have that impact.

## Ⓖ Managing Paraprofessionals

When in library school, the term paraprofessional can seem pretty clear-cut. They are people who don't have a master's degree in library science (MLS) but work in libraries. Makes sense, right? In the workplace, this term becomes more problematic. Not every professional in a library has an MLS. There are usually exempt professionals working in IT and business services, for instance. Likewise, not everyone with an MLS is in a "professional" role, especially if librarians have faculty status, which is a very specific category at universities, applied to only certain job lines and totally distinct from staff. Additionally, though there are many people who technically fall into a "paraprofessional" job category, they may have decades of experience and do many tasks that require a deep, detailed understanding of library operations. All this is to say, there is not really a good term for the vast category of library employees who don't hold an MLS, and though they are referred to as paraprofessionals here, that's not really the right term. There isn't a better one to differentiate between various kinds of employees.

This group may be different in several important ways from librarians, who are discussed later. For one, some don't intend to make their career in libraries. Others may choose to make their career in libraries but don't want to pursue an MLS. Still others might have an MLS, or aspire to obtain one, but aren't currently working in a role that requires it. As a result, there are different approaches to working with each type of paraprofessional.

For paraprofessionals that view their role in the library as a step toward some other goal, training in transferable skills and more general opportunities for professional development can be the most useful approach. Explaining how their current role and job responsibilities prepare them to achieve their ultimate aspirations can be effective. In this case, the supervising librarian is a tour guide of sorts, explaining the nuances of libraries to someone new to them, and probably just visiting. While it's good to avoid pressuring this kind of employee into taking on more responsibility if it makes them uncomfortable, suggesting ways that they could grow and advance in the library is always a good idea, especially if they show a particular knack. Many people who have made long careers in libraries started out pursuing another aspiration, only to find that the library is exactly where they wanted to be. Just because an employee conveys that they don't plan to stay in libraries, doesn't mean that they won't change their mind later.

Paraprofessionals who have a career in libraries but don't plan to get an MLS can be some of the most challenging for librarians, and new librarians in particular. Often, these employees have many years of experience, and know more about the day-to-day operations of the library than the newly minted MLS. They don't plan to get an MLS and tend to resent the implication that the graduate degree overrules their lived experience, as well they should. These employees are colleagues who fill important roles in our institutions, and they should be approached this way. They can be a manager's best ally, if the manager takes time to grow the relationship in the right way.

There are a few steps to ensure a strong, collegial relationship with this category of paraprofessional. First, respect their institutional, technical, and professional knowledge. They may well know a lot more than a new supervisor. Approach them in a way that denotes that this is understood, and be open to learning from them. Second, treat them like colleagues rather than subordinates, because that's what they are. Third, recognize the value in what they do, and promote their professional development. With tight travel and training budgets, sometimes they can get overlooked when these opportunities are doled out. Try to ensure that this does not happen. Fourth, and finally, find ways to ensure that they have career trajectories of their own that do not require additional schooling.

Paraprofessionals who have an MLS, or who plan to get one, are very similar to early-career librarians. Try to think of opportunities that promote leadership and growth toward a librarian position. For universities where the librarians are faculty, this entails the opportunity to publish and perform research, as well as possible teaching opportunities. For other kinds of libraries, this might mean management experiences or positions on leadership teams. The key here is to think about the kinds of responsibilities that employers look for when they hire a professional librarian. Give these employees duties that correlate with key competencies.

As mentioned above, in addition to paraprofessionals, professionals from other fields often work in libraries, such as those who handle IT, business functions, or human resources. They have their own trajectories for building careers and developing professionally. Be aware of the expectations in these professions, and support these staff appropriately. Keeping these employees happy is important because they can be difficult to rehire. They may be working for less money than they could get elsewhere because they like the library environment.

## Managing Librarians

When managing fellow librarians, the best style to use is often peer to peer. The idea here is to approach these situations as more collegial than hierarchical. This approach ensures that the librarians know they are respected, and their professional expertise and insights are valued. This also promotes a flexible and open environment where professional staff and faculty feel free to share questions, concerns, and thoughts about decisions made in the library.

It's helpful to think of librarians in the same way as other faculty at universities—focused experts with a certain aversion to hierarchical structures. This is because faculty are super experts in their respective fields. This level of expertise has afforded them autonomy and authority, even if they aren't leaders in their department. In this model, department chairs are one among many authorities in their units, and are often thought of as coordinators of human resources rather than "bosses." So too, faculty governance is a cherished principle in higher education, one enshrined in accreditation standards. Faculty are given primary authority in areas directly related to their expertise, such as curriculum development, grading policies, and other issues related to the quality of their courses. As professionals, faculty are recognized as leaders, even if they don't have leadership positions.

Like faculty, librarians should be respected as autonomous professionals with expertise in specific areas and authority over processes and services, even when they are not in leadership positions. They should share responsibility for the department and decisions made related to its management. Though it is easy to fall into the trap of thinking of employees as subordinates, it is vitally important that they are treated like equals, though there are times when unilateral decisions need to be made. If the other librarians are treated as equals and feel valued, the occasional unilateral decision is much easier to accept and respect.

Keep in mind that not every employee is going to respond well to this approach, because some may try to take advantage of collegiality. Still, at the professional level, this is a much smaller concern—people who have dedicated themselves to a career in libraries, enough so to earn a master's degree, are generally reliable. The key here is goal setting—making expectations clear early, and often, so that professional staff are never surprised by a good or a bad evaluation.

When managing professionals, mentoring remains important. Remember that librarians, and really all employees, are at different stages in their careers. This means the approach varies depending on where they are. Early-career librarians, for instance, are being inducted into the profession, and they probably require some hand-holding, as well as some confidence-building. Approach them with a frank assessment of the field as it stands, but also encouragement. Don't be too cynical, or too optimistic. At this stage, maintaining a balanced outlook is ideal.

By mid-career, the way a librarian is going to distinguish him- or herself becomes clear. Broadly speaking, most librarians are leaders in some sense by mid-career, though different people lead in different ways. Some excel in professional service, such as for the American Library Association (ALA); some really shine in scholarship; some are at their best when they are doing the work, such as a really stellar instruction librarian; and some show promise as future administrators. Mentoring those who want to follow in one's own footsteps is easy. Mentoring those who are going to follow a path totally different is much harder. Be as thoughtful and supportive as possible. Don't expect that everyone wants to be a head of public services or assistant director. Many librarians want to advance by becoming better as practitioners. The most important thing about working with mid-career librarians is focusing them in the direction where they can "hit their stride" professionally, and giving them the space and opportunities to achieve that career high.

For late-career librarians, some managers see them as people who are "winding down," but this is really a reductive approach. Many late-career librarians want to try something new before they retire, or as a second job after they have retired once. This might mean moving to a new kind of a position, a new area of the library, or a new library altogether. These librarians are great hires, even if their experience isn't in the same niche as the position they are applying for, because they already know the profession and the expectations. They also already have leadership positions in their background and become natural leaders in a library, even if they aren't managers. If they are in an existing position, the hardest part is keeping them challenged and interested. They are often so acclimated to their job that it doesn't hold many surprises. A supervisor has to work extra hard to make sure the work remains engaging. Special projects that require working across departments can be especially good for this type of employee. Whatever the situation, remember that late-career librarians are not just counting down days until retirement—they are there to grow as professionals, just like all the rest.

This highlights one particular hallmark of a professional employee: continued development and contributions to the broader field. Though every employee can develop and contribute, professional employees should be expected to do so. No matter the type of institution, helping guide professional employees to become involved in librarianship as a field is a big part of managing them. For institutions of higher education, this can mean helping library faculty to create a research agenda and publish—coauthoring with them on their first publication is one way to do this. At public institutions and schools, this means urging employees to find opportunities to take courses or present at conferences.

## Human Resources

One common view of the human resources department is that it exists to protect the interests of an institution, and not the employee. This isn't necessarily true, especially if excellent human resource professionals have everyone's best interest at heart. Whatever the case, though, human resources is most certainly there for managers—to help them do their best, and also to ensure that they don't make a wrong step. Rely on them! When considering firing, disciplining, promoting, or commending staff, the first conversation should be with human resources, and not the staff themselves. In good times, human resources are able to identify what resources are available to reward and retain the best employees. In the bad times, they guide a manager through the many issues that can arise.

Another reason to keep human resources close is that there are all sorts of rules, regulations, and laws that managers need to follow in order to remain aligned with the requirements of an institution. These include things like compensation structures, employee disciplinary procedures, Americans with Disabilities Act (ADA) requirements, and other issues. There are probably more of these rules and regulations than it is possible to remember. Helpful human resources personnel make sure managers follow them. Go to them for consultation before a mistake is made, not after. For a better understanding of these kinds of rules and requirements, *Library Management 101* discusses this topic at some length (Hussey and Velasquez 2019). Keep in mind that, generally, a local HR department trains new managers and guides them about the policies in their organization.

Human resources can also provide training and advice related to mentorship. As mentioned above, not everyone is open to being mentored by their manager. Sometimes differences in personality or leadership styles preclude the formation of this kind of relationship. Human resources can help find creative solutions to ensure that no employee languishes. Though the work of George Kuh (1995; 2008) specifically relates to student workers, it is true that all employees who feel a real connection to the institution, and to somebody at the institution who can help them reach the next level professionally—even when that person isn't their manager—will do better work, stay longer, and be more likely to succeed.

## Key Points

- People remember managers who are mentors.
- Student work prepares students for professional life after college.
- Student work also makes students more involved on campus.
- Paraprofessionals are a highly variable group in libraries, and management should be tailored to their specific career goals.
- Professional librarians should be treated more as colleagues than employees.

- Librarians must be encouraged to participate in the larger professional conversation.
- Human Resources exists to ensure managers are aligned with the law and institutional mandates. Take advantage of HR expertise.

## References

Brustein, Darrah. 2018. "How Warren Buffett and Steven Spielberg Used Strategic Relationships to Launch Their Careers." *Forbes*, January 10. https://www.forbes.com/sites/darrahbrustein/2018/06/10/how-warren-buffett-and-steven-spielberg-used-strategic-relationships-to-launch-their-careers/?sh=2cf169cb267a.

Gallo, Carmine. 2017. "Steven Spielberg's First Boss Made This Promise That Unleashed the Director's Creativity." *Forbes*, October 9. https://www.forbes.com/sites/carminegallo/2017/10/09/steven-spielbergs-first-boss-made-this-promise-that-unleashed-the-directors-creativity/?sh=1d89f65a46d7.

Hussey, Lisa K., and Diane L. Velasquez, eds. 2019. *Library Management 101: A Practical Guide*. Chicago: ALA Editions. Kindle.

Kuh, George. 1995. "The Other Curriculum: Out-of-Class Experiences Associated with Student Learning and Personal Development." *Journal of Higher Education* 66 (2): 123–55. JSTOR.

———. 2008. *High Impact Educational Practices*. Washington DC: Association of American Colleges & Universities.

Lewis, Andy, and Maya Anderman. 2016. "Discovered by Spielberg: How a Lucky Encounter with the Director Launched These 6 Stars." *Hollywood Reporter*, May 6. https://www.hollywoodreporter.com/news/discovered-by-spielberg-a-lucky-891580.

Reale, Michelle. 2013. *Mentoring and Managing Students in the Academic Library*. Chicago: ALA Editions. Kindle.

# Coordinating Resources

NAPOLEON BONAPARTE IS REMEMBERED as one of history's great generals. In many ways, he invented modern warfare through strategic and tactical innovations. One of these was the creation of supply chains that ensured his armies remained well fed, stocked, and paid throughout campaigns. His soldiers didn't have to spend all of their time scouring the countryside, subsisting on what they could pillage or scavenge, as earlier armies had. Well-fed soldiers stay healthier, and can focus on preparing for battle rather than their next meal. Soldiers who are cared for are also, in turn, loyal to their commander (Schneid 2005). This was true in Napoleon's case. His men were deeply devoted to him, allowing him to inspire them to fight harder and better. Napoleon's major military mistake came when he invaded Russia in 1812. As many students of military history already know, the vast, open land of Russia, combined with its harsh climate, make it difficult to invade. Large armies can't live off the land, since it doesn't produce enough to feed them. The scorched-earth tactics of the Russian military exacerbated this problem, since they burned crops and cities to halt resupply of foreign armies. Napoleon's invasion failed, in part, for the same reasons many of his other campaigns had succeeded: supply chains. The troops didn't have the food and provisions they needed to hold Moscow after the Russians burned it to the ground (Zamoyski 2005).

While middle managers in libraries are not military generals tasked, as Napoleon was, with ensuring half a million troops are fed and supplied in a myriad of complex situations, there is an important principle buried in this story. Leaders who get their subordinates the resources they need to do the job inspire loyalty and respect. Those who fail are likely to face problems with morale, and possibly defeat. This is particularly difficult for many middle managers, who have limited resources as well as little control over how the budget is allocated. Librarians enter middle management with a million brilliant ideas, but when they start to try and make those changes, they realize they have little control, and moreover, their staff have many, many needs that are difficult to meet with current funds. These middle managers face a three-pronged problem: they must get their employees what they need, and make a real mark on the department as the new leader, while having little control over how the money is allocated. In other words, this chapter might better be called budgeting without a budget. While it might seem like a manager has no recourse in this situation, there are things that can be done to satisfy the constraints of all three prongs of the problem.

## Definitions

Donation in kind: A donation of goods or services, instead of a monetary amount.

Endowed staff or faculty line: An employee line that is funded by the annual return on investment for a pot of donated money.

Endowment: A monetary or in-kind donation. An endowment is usually indefinitely perpetuated in support of some entity, project, institution, or organization.

Indirect funds: Funds that support the administrative and facility overhead incurred as the result of a grant, usually represented as a percentage of the overall grant funds.

## Making Resource Decisions

Though middle managers might not have budget control, they probably have resource control. This means that they govern where their employees are going to put their energy. They also recommend the software those employees use to do it. They determine what supplies and technology are needed to achieve success. They guide the ship, even if they don't control the budget. The key is understanding how to navigate a skiff without manning the rudder.

## Changing Positions

The human resources in a unit are probably the most expensive thing under a middle manager's control. Remember that each employee line has two expenses associated with it: salary and benefits. If the institution is similar to the majority of others, getting a new employee line, out of nothing and with no outside funding, is pretty tricky. This is compounded by the fact that the library is competing with every other unit in the university, city, or county to get that new employee. Is the administration going to determine that a new archivist is more necessary than a new firefighter, teacher, or social worker? That's a really tough question, and the answer often doesn't favor the library.

What a unit does have is existing employee lines. When people leave, there is a good opportunity to revise a position in order to get something new. This is not going to help if there aren't enough people to achieve what is already required, with no room for change. Such a case necessitates a different strategy. If the problem is, however, that the unit doesn't have the right person to achieve its goals, the manager can always make a new position out of an existing budgeted line, which won't require increased funding. Never fill a position straight off without reviewing it. Though it is genuinely unfortunate to lose good employees, the one silver lining is that the unit gets to rethink what the staff member does, and potentially make a new position. Even if the manager doesn't have control over the budget, they almost certainly have control over the position descriptions and duties for employees. This provides the autonomy to make a new decision even without budget control.

Additionally, there are more creative options, some of which are better than others, that might be possible if they are budget-neutral, meaning they won't cost any additional money. Breaking an existing full-time position into two part-time positions, for instance, saves money on benefits, but can result in more staff time. The drawback is that the position won't be as attractive, and so it is harder to hire and keep someone reliable. Further, getting back a full-time position once it is gone is much harder than keeping a full-time position. This is because full-time positions are subject to many more laws and regulations, not to mention that they usually come with benefits, and are probably closely controlled by the larger organization. There is also the ethical consideration—if somebody could get benefits and a full-time job, is there a social obligation to do so?

Hiring at a lower level can also save money. The obvious implication of this is that one could hire a student worker instead of a paraprofessional, or a paraprofessional instead of a librarian, but most organizations have levels for paraprofessionals and librarians. One could hire a librarian I instead of a librarian IV, for instance, without changing the professional status. This makes the most sense in situations where especially competent employees worked their way up into positions that only they could fill. The job description has become so packed with duties, and so convoluted, that it would be difficult to hire anyone else who could do it. Money is saved, and the library has an easier time hiring someone new if the position is downgraded. This should be presented to the director as a way of saving money to get a part-timer or something else the unit needs, rather than to free up money for the library at large. Have a reason why it only works if the leftover funds are used in the way the unit needs in case the director asks for the money back. Though sometimes a budget cut or other crisis might require making such changes and giving up the saved funds, in a normal year a manager should always present money-saving opportunities as a way to shift funds within a unit, to prioritize other goals. If it isn't presented in this way, the director is liable to reclaim the money and shift it to another area of the library, which is a net loss for the middle manager and not the aim of these strategies.

## Let's Make a Deal

Another approach to working within existing resources to get the department what it needs might be called "let's make a deal." Usually, this strategy is useful when two different areas need something, but neither of them can get everything they want with the existing resources. Let's say Dennis has a part-timer that he's afraid he will lose if he can't convert the position to full time. Maybe the part-timer does reserves and gets really busy at the beginning of the semester, but is relatively free near the end. Mary, on the other hand, needs someone to help with interlibrary loan (ILL), which gets extra busy during the last two-thirds of the semester. She really needs a full-time position, but she only has enough money for a part-timer. Maybe between the two of them, there's enough funding to create one full-time line, if Dennis and Mary are willing to share. They might both want a full-time position, but this way, they can at least get help for their employees—Dennis's staff member goes to full time, and Mary gets assistance for her ILL librarian.

These deals are even better when the managers work them out before the director gets involved. Directors are so glad when managers see these opportunities and take the initiative to work together. This is to say that, if one controls resources that are valuable to someone else, this sort of horse trading can be an effective way to get what is needed. In most cases, the boss is thrilled with the negotiated solution, because he or she probably spends a lot of time pondering how to make sure everyone has what they require—the director likely never reaches that goal, which is an unending source of frustration. Being proactive is a huge help.

## ⊚ Getting Donations

Another method to get needed, but elusive, resources is through soliciting donations. One warning: when donations are discussed, there are some people who act as though they are a panacea for all of a library's problems, as though suddenly a manager will be sitting on piles of gold like some dragon in a cave if only they go out and ask. This might be true for those with a giant endowment or a local, sympathetic billionaire. For those at regional state schools, small community colleges, or branch libraries in small towns, this is usually not the case. Librarians are more likely to be working at a branch campus in a strip mall between an Aldi and an insurance broker than an R1 university with a mega-endowment. Do not think that donations are going to save the library, because they probably won't. They might not even fill holes in the operating budget. What they can do is launch truly interesting projects, and that is most definitely something. Donations are especially viable in situations where the goal is to fund a new or continuing program that is seen as particularly valuable to some subset of a local community, not as a way to cover ongoing library expenses.

Remember that donations are not only monetary. Donations in kind, which include goods and services, are also quite helpful. Libraries often deal with in-kind donations of books or valuable archival collections, but all types of things can be donated. Technology, supplies, or other types of equipment are examples of potential donations. For a special program or to create a new service, these kinds of items are especially valuable because they save a lot of money on the upfront costs. They are attractive to donors because they are one-time expenses, so they don't require an ongoing commitment or the creation of an endowment.

Though every situation is different, as mentioned above, big donors are usually attracted to a specific project or service, not to the library in a broad sense. The possible exception to this is a naming right to the library facility or spaces, which is often granted as the result of a substantial, more general donation to the institution. Library sponsorship programs, which solicit smaller donations, also often go toward more general operating expenses or renovations to facilities. In either case, middle managers probably won't be working with people who are looking at these kinds of donations. As a result, middle managers should focus on specific services or projects that might be viewed favorably by potential charitable community members or groups. Have an idea of what kind of donations are needed to set up this project or that service—financial resources, equipment, or supplies. Then look around at the entities and individuals in the community that regularly fund similar causes. For smaller projects that require food or other supplies, big-box stores and grocery stores are good places to start because they usually give either in-kind or financial support to various community-supportive causes.

Keep in mind that a large donation that sustains a project for years, including wages and salaries, is unlikely right off the bat. These kinds of endowments take years to get and build, because a project has to demonstrate its value and find the right donor. Also, many donors do not support salaries. Big-box stores and grocery stores, for instance, often only provide equipment and supplies. For programs that require outside funding for both wages and supplies, two donors might be necessary, or a combination of donations and grants. This can be tricky, because some donors prefer to be the only contributor, so know the details involved when accepting resources. Either way, the best bet is to try to pay for the salaries out of the existing budget, as those are often the hardest to fund through donations. This is especially true if a project requires an endowed salary—one that is going to be paid through the annual return on investment for a pot of donated money. For this kind of donation, the endowment for the salary must be many times larger than the annual salary itself in order to support a staff or faculty line. One-time donations of money or resources are much easier to obtain.

The biggest thing to remember when looking for resources is that the organization probably has someone who manages donations, and this person should be the first stop. He or she might have ideas for who in the community would be interested in supporting the project. This person also knows all of the rules and regulations related to donations for the organization, and can ensure that potential contributions won't eat into an already existing source of funding, so the project doesn't negatively impact another department that depends on charitable funds.

In addition, the library likely has a friends group that should be kept in the loop. Many friends groups hold big annual charitable events, like book sales or dinners. These support the libraries with which they are affiliated. Even if they don't have funds to give to a project, they can probably plan such an event. These kinds of occasions are helpful in raising capital, though they may also cost more than they bring in, so the budget must be closely scrutinized if this is the chosen path.

Though seeking donations might seem daunting, don't be afraid! The worst that can happen is someone will say no. There are likely far more resources out there than is immediately apparent, and these can allow significant expansions of the library's services. Also remember that some donations have so many strings attached that they aren't worth it—for instance, the donation of funds for an engineering collection at a library, contingent on the university offering a PhD in engineering. The cost, in this case, would almost certainly be way more than the benefit of the donation. The organization would probably graciously turn down such an offer.

## ⊚ Finding Grants

Like donations, grant funding can be a valuable way to fund specific projects or services. In order to appeal to granting organizations, have a clear idea of the project or service, the impact it will have, the duration of the grant funding, and the budget for items to be funded. While having a well-defined proposal with measurable goals is helpful when asking for donations, it is essential when going for grants. Also, keep in mind that, as with donations, a grant is not likely to support the day-to-day operations of a library. A clear project or service that aligns with the goals of the grant and granting organization is required to compete for funding. That said, grants often come with something called "indirect funds" that do support the administrative and facility overhead involved with the grant. These funds help the library's bottom line.

There are lots of online resources that discuss finding grants, including Grants.gov, which is free, and Foundation Center, which is not. Federal and state governments are probably the best place to start. Usually, federal grants are more challenging to get than state grants. They also often require an established program or project with a few years of data. State grants are generally easier, but they tend to be smaller and shorter in duration. As with anything, these are extreme generalizations that don't apply across the board. Also look at organizations with a charitable interest in areas related to the funding being sought. For instance, Honda counts technological and engineering education among its many grantable interests. The HEB grocery chain in the state of Texas is actively involved in the promotion of literacy, and a lot of their grant funding is related to that goal. When searching for a grant, look to see who has been awarded funding in the past, and ask them about their experience. There may also be a training or other authoritative resource related to applying for and receiving the grant in question.

After identifying an interesting funding source, look for other people in the organization who have received grants. There are probably going to be at least a few. Among those people, find someone who really knows about grant-writing—the person everyone else who has gotten a grant talked to for support and encouragement. Become friends with this person, who will be a valuable resource. Grant-writing is extremely specialized, with its own expectations and requirements. People pay a lot of money for grant-writing seminars and services. If this information is available for free from someone who really knows how to do it well, the library is lucky indeed. If no one is really good at grant-writing, try *The Only Grant-Writing Book You'll Ever Need* by Ellen Karsh and Arlen Sue Fox (2019).

Remember, when trying to garner resources for special projects and new programs, as with anything in life: no risk, no reward. Spending two months working on a detailed grant application might end up being two months of wasted time, but a project or program won't get off the ground without it. Also remember that, while grant funding and donations are often limited in how the money provided can be spent, technology and other equipment purchased through grants usually remain with the library after the grant is over. New equipment, such as laptops or iPads for staff, can be very useful.

This points to one important thing about resource coordination in general. With so many big ideas for the future, many new middle managers with lean resources prioritize new projects and initiatives, sometimes excluding the day-to-day technology and equipment needs of staff. These managers do this at their own peril. The best solution is a donation or grant that purchases this equipment for a special project, which can then be used by staff for various purposes after the grant period ends—that's one of the best features of this type of funding. Even when a grant or donation isn't forthcoming, putting the needs of staff over some more ambitious goal is sometimes necessary. Buying librarians new laptops so they don't have to work on ten-year-old systems, or buying a new CoLibri machine when the old one breaks down, can create goodwill with staff and let them know that the manager cares. Understanding that basic work needs matter makes a difference, as Napoleon's many military successes show. Make room in the budget when it's needed, even if that means putting a big, new idea on the back burner for a while. The staff will appreciate it, and repay the kindness tenfold in the quality of their work.

## ◎ Key Points

- Though middle managers might not have control over their budgets, they do have control over resources, including positions.
- Middle managers should be creative in the way they manage these resources.
- Donations and grants can help supplement budgets for middle managers, especially for new projects and programs.

## ◎ References

Karsh, Ellen, and Arlen Sue Fox. 2019. *The Only Grant-Writing Book You'll Ever Need*, 5th edition. New York: Basic Books.

Schneid, Frederick. 2005. *Napoleon's Conquest of Europe: The War of the Third Coalition*. Westport, CT: Praeger.

Zamoyski, Adam. 2005. *1812: Napoleon's Fatal March on Moscow*. London: Harper Perennial. Kindle.

# Strategic Planning and Assessment

THIS CHAPTER RETURNS TO FAMILIAR THEMES: planning; how plans are, in some sense, useless; and why planning is imperative. Strategic planning is the process whereby managers determine overarching goals to shape and direct their decision-making. All organizational assessment is linked to and based on strategic planning. Therefore, having a sound strategic plan shapes all assessment activities carried out by a unit. The centrality of the strategic plan cannot be overstated.

The definition of strategy used throughout this chapter is taken from Henry Mintzberg, the Cleghorn Professor of Management Studies at McGill University. Strategy is, simply put, "a pattern in a stream of decisions" (1978, 935). Every manager is faced with an unending series of choices about how the department is managed and where it is headed. Strategy is a pattern of decision-making toward a single set of goals. For instance, a library that preferences electronic materials over print would enact that strategy as a pattern of electronic purchases. A library with a goal of producing information-literate students would take opportunities to teach a credit-hour information literacy course, even if such a course requires a big outlay of resources. Strategy is the pattern of decisions that lead to success in terms of the library's short- and long-term objectives.

Thinking of strategy as a pattern of decisions helps to understand strategic planning. This is a big word that is not as complicated as it might seem. Strategic planning is simply a process where leaders and other stakeholders decide what the objectives should be for all of the decisions they make. In other words, where should the organization be steered by the choices made today and tomorrow? This is preferable to making decisions as questions arise, because it lends intentionality to the process. Having a strategy helps leaders say no to appealing opportunities that would take resources away from the main goals of the organization, and say yes to things that might seem difficult or uninteresting when they further these same goals.

As an example, a library might be approached by an arts group with a request to host weekly luncheons featuring classical musicians in the community. The library would provide the catering, and the arts group would pay the musicians. Though this may be a potentially popular program, it is also likely to be expensive. Let's say that, in this case, it does not directly impact the achievement of the library's main goals, which are centered on providing high-quality materials for the community. Though this is an attractive program idea, the library probably shouldn't pursue it, because it's resource-intensive and not directly correlated to its mission. On the other hand, a library might be approached by a local newspaper that is going out of business. Though the city library has never digitized historical resources before, the newspaper would like to transfer their physical archives, as well as the copyright for these archives, to the library. This is also resource-intensive, but if the library's mission focuses on providing access to high-quality information, it may agree to take over the physical resources and to digitize them, even though this is a totally new area. As these examples show, strategic plans guide hard yeses, and hard nos, to ensure that the library is fulfilling its primary purpose.

Though the director of a library is usually the most actively involved in strategic planning, middle managers generally participate. As a result, they must be able to think strategically about how they are guiding and growing their unit, aligned with the larger goals of the organization, and also the smaller goals that the manager has set forth. Moreover, middle managers are frequently required to do formalized assessments and show impact for the work done by their unit, and these assessments correlate with the high-level strategy of the organization. Think of strategic plans like nesting dolls. The main plan for the city or the university encompasses all of the smaller plans across the organization. The academic master plan, for instance, aligns with the larger one put out by the university, and the library's smaller one aligns with the academic master plan. This is true down to the strategy of individual units, which is the smallest doll at the heart of planning and assessment efforts. This is extremely important, because the work done at the unit level eventually helps the organization as a whole meet its objectives. A middle manager who remembers this, and can show how his or her unit is directly contributing to the achievement of high-level organizational objectives, is in a much better position than one who can't.

## Definitions

Assessment plan: An annual measure of whether a unit has achieved its objectives.

Guiding principles: Statements that lay out shared values and beliefs, shaping how business is done at every level.

Imperative: A concept that defines the areas that objectives fall under.

Mission: The overarching goal of an organization or unit.

Objectives: Goals to be reached during an established period of time.

Performance indicators: Clearly measurable milestones with associated due dates that mark success for strategies.

Stakeholder: Someone with an interest or stake in the institution.

Strategic planning: A process where leaders and other stakeholders decide what the objectives should be for all of the decisions they make.

Strategies: Concrete actions that the library will take to achieve objectives.

SWOT analysis: The process of figuring out what an organization's strengths, weaknesses, opportunities, and threats are.

# The Strategic Planning Process

As mentioned above, strategic planning is the process whereby an organization determines a plan for the next several years, and determines how resources are allocated to achieve the goals laid out in this plan. Strategic planning processes can vary, but they usually involve the following steps:

1. Reviewing the mission and guiding principles to ensure that they remain consistent with the organization as it currently exists.
2. Gathering information.
3. Identifying objectives or goals to be reached during the established period of time.
4. Identifying strategies or activities to help achieve these goals, and ways to measure whether the strategies are successful.
5. Creating assessment methods for the strategic plan. This is likely linked to the strategies identified above, and should include a cycle for review at least annually.
6. Allowing stakeholders to review, provide input, and approve the plan.
7. Implementing the plan.

As these steps suggest, the strategic planning process is reiterative. Once the plan is created, it doesn't sit on the shelf for years without further consideration. A strategic plan is a living document that is reviewed and assessed annually, in order to ensure that it remains relevant to the needs of the organization. This chapter discusses each step, including opportunities to review and reshape the plan as it is pursued.

Note that, though this process is usually completed by a small group of people, the effort as a whole incorporates the input of all members of the wider community. It can't take place in a silo. For this reason, in order to ensure that the plan is effective, it's important to include many kinds of patrons, the staff in the unit, upper administration, and other types of stakeholders. Leaders might believe they have an accurate picture of what is happening, but sometimes a manager is too close to the work to really recognize what is meaningful.

Another thing to remember about strategic planning across all levels of the organization is that resources are often allocated in direct alignment with such plans. In other words, if a unit is asking for new funding for a children's librarian or an off-site storage facility, it has a much better chance of getting that funding if it directly supports the organization's master strategic plan. This makes good sense, because the strategic plan is the road map for achieving the major long-term goals of the organization. Every other lower-level strategic plan across the organization aligns with and supports these long-term goals—this is the nesting doll discussed earlier. New funding is often allocated first to priorities listed in the highest-level plan, because these are the most important. Having library priorities in high-level strategic plans for the city or university is extremely important because of this direct impact on the budget.

Finally, remember that these goals are unique to an institution. Some people have the idea that every library is essentially the same—buying books, helping people find things, and providing access to resources. In reality, every library is different, as is every institution served by a library. A small, rural public library is going to be quite different than a large, metropolitan research library. That research library will have totally different goals than a community college library serving mostly nontraditional students. When planning strategically, finding and supporting the nuances that make the institution different helps the library succeed. This is to say that libraries shouldn't simply recreate a plan from another institution. For each library, planning should be specific and unique, reflecting all of the things that distinguish it.

## Step 1: Reviewing the Mission

The first step in any strategic planning process is reviewing the mission and guiding principles of the organization. Though many organizations complete this review by determining that their mission and guiding principles are sound, others may decide that they need to be revised. A mission is the overarching purpose of an organization or unit. Usually, the mission is stated in one or two sentences, though not always. Everything done by an organization—and as a result, by the leaders of the organization—should support the mission. Guiding principles are statements that lay out the shared values and beliefs, shaping how business is done at every level. Usually the mission and guiding principles work together to provide the framework to understand why an organization exists, as well as how it operates. Because both of these documents are fundamental, they must accurately reflect the institution. The mission guides strategic planning, and if it isn't accurate, the chosen strategies likely won't work.

There is no one definition of what a mission contains, though it always describes the main purpose of an organization. Usually, it also explains how an institution achieves this and the scope of the work done, such as local, regional, national, or international. Good missions are unique, and they define what is special about an organization. A library with a mission to "check out books to as many members of the local community as possible" probably identifies its main goal accurately, but gives little indication about what sets the library apart. Many institutions establish a mission early in their tenure, and then don't revise it. This is a mistake, especially if the organization has undergone many changes over time. For instance, a library that still cites print books as its raison d'etre is probably due for an update. A mission needs to change as the organization itself changes.

There are many ways to review a mission and vision, but the key is to gather prominent leaders and stakeholders together to ensure everyone has input. The best way to look at the mission and principles is to break them down into each constituent part, and go through them to ensure they are all still true, accurate, and essential. As with the example above, though the library might continue to buy print, perhaps that isn't the defining element it once was.

If any aspects of the mission are no longer accurate, or if there seems to be a strong general sense among stakeholders and leaders that it's time to do a full revision, the process used should encompass the whole organization. One strategy is to have members of each unit send words and phrases that define core elements of what they do, and then correlate these responses until clear, core activities become evident. Another strategy is to have different working groups write proposed missions, and then come together to choose which best fits the organization as a whole, perhaps even combining the top elements of each. Though these are just two possible approaches, they both employ groups of people across the institution to form the new mission. Ensuring that any change or revision flows from the library stakeholders is essential.

## Step 2: Gathering Information

The biggest activity that takes place when gathering information is the SWOT analysis, though that is not the only one. A SWOT analysis is the process of figuring out what an organization's strengths, weaknesses, opportunities and threats are. The strengths and weaknesses are internal to the organization, and can be defined as what an institution is really good at and what it is really bad at. Opportunities and threats are external to the organization, and are the prospects on the horizon that would allow growth, as well as the dangers that the organization faces outside of its scope of influence from competitors, funding organizations, or other forces that could damage it. The goal of a SWOT analysis is to survey a great number of people who are affiliated with the institution to get a broad idea of how they perceive it. This allows the strategic planning group to find the most frequent themes related to each of the SWOT elements, and to reckon with these in the objectives and strategies that ultimately make up the plan. The SWOT analysis is, then, one of the main ways that an organization gathers data to inform the formulation of a strategic plan.

A SWOT analysis can be done in many different ways. The most common method is a survey with open-ended questions sent to staff, students, patrons, and other stakeholders. Open-ended, qualitative questions are most useful because the goal is to allow respondents to share their own feelings about the library, rather than to shape their answers by limiting responses to predetermined multiple-choice questions. Focus groups might be another way of performing this type of analysis, though the anonymity that a survey allows is probably more conducive to honest answers about weaknesses and threats, especially when responses might be unflattering.

Once the surveys are returned, the group working on the strategic plan goes through each response category, and picks out recurring patterns. For instance, under weaknesses, patrons might repeatedly mention issues related to customer service, though they might not all say the same thing. Some might mention the attitude of service desk staff, where others say they didn't receive a timely answer to their question. These responses would all be categorized under the larger category of customer service, to allow for the most important concerns and opportunities to influence the creation of objectives and strategies.

Beyond the SWOT analysis, the data-gathering phase should also involve a survey of the broader terrain and context in which the organization is operating. Information about funding patterns and long-term projections, population and demographic growth, trends and changes that libraries are undergoing in a broader sense, and the strategic objectives of the larger institution should be gathered during this stage. This data contributes to a fuller and more nuanced understanding of the big picture at hand relative to the library. This big picture is the key to strong strategic planning. A library in the Sun Belt, for instance, that is facing a significant increase in population over the next twenty years is going to have a very different strategic plan than one in the Rust Belt with an aging population and collapsing tax base. Though their SWOT analyses might pull out the same strengths, weaknesses, opportunities, and threats, the realities facing libraries due to the contexts in which they operate have a big impact on how they plan for the future.

## Step 3: Identifying Objectives

Once data is gathered, the group working on the strategic plan analyzes it. As mentioned above, this entails putting responses into categories to determine the recurrent themes that seem to resonate the most with stakeholders. The objectives grow out of these themes. In a strategic plan, objectives are the overarching goals for the organization during the stated period of time—most strategic plans run between five and ten years. One key is to avoid having too many objectives. When there are too many, they can be overwhelming, and keep the staff from focusing on the ones that are most important. Objectives might be organized under larger headings, such as "excellent customer service" or "high-quality materials" to help link them to the larger themes on which the library will focus.

Objectives should be broad but also measurable. Examples of objectives might be:

- Prepare information-literate citizens that evaluate the quality of news they encounter in their everyday lives.
- Use meaningful materials and programming to promote literacy from early childhood to adulthood.
- Create an informed citizenry capable of meaningful participation in the democratic process.
- Support the ongoing research and learning of students, faculty, and staff through instruction and access to academic materials.

This is a short list of potential objectives that might appear in different types of strategic plans for libraries. These objectives are not statements of clear assessment goals, such as to increase circulation by 5 percent annually or to have students reach a certain pass rate on a measure of information literacy. Rather, these are broader goals that encompass a set of strategies, or activities, that can be measured.

Be clear when writing objectives. Generally, objectives are constructed with a verb or action, followed by information related to that action, such as "create information-literate students," "answer questions satisfactorily," and so forth. Objectives don't have to be elaborate, though they do need to be detailed enough to suggests strategies, or activities, that could be used to achieve them.

The purpose of objectives is to define the larger aims of the library, organized under categories of concern, sometimes called imperatives. If customer service is a clear weakness following the SWOT analysis, the imperative that would follow would be "excellent customer service," and under this imperative there would be several overarching customer service objectives, such as "provide timely answers to customer questions." The imperative defines the area that objectives fall under, and the objectives are the goals related to the imperative. Each imperative should have a few objectives. A plan should have a limited, manageable, and meaningful number of imperatives.

## Step 4: Identifying Strategies

Strategies are the activities that are proposed to achieve the objectives. Strategies are concrete actions that the library will take. For instance, if the objective is to create information-literate citizens, the strategy or concrete action might be to "provide funding to support information literacy programming across the organization" or "create a one-credit information literacy course for all incoming freshmen." These are concrete actions the library will take to reach the objective. These strategies are often based directly on recurrent themes in the SWOT analysis, such as identified opportunities or weaknesses. Strategies should be measurable in the sense that they have correlated data points that can show whether or not they were successful. Each objective should have a few strategies associated with it, but not so many that it becomes overwhelming.

## Step 5: Creating Assessment Measures

Once the objectives and strategies are identified, performance indicators should be associated with each objective. These performance indicators are the assessment measures to help show whether the objectives have been met. They are clearly measurable milestones with associated due dates. They correlate with the strategies. For instance, if the strategy is to create a one-credit information literacy course, the performance measure might be to have 75 percent of incoming freshmen pass this course with a C or better by 2025. Another might be to have 90 percent of students who complete this course pass a standardized assessment related to information literacy by the third year the course is offered. These performance indicators are reviewed and reported on every year to measure how successful the organization is in achieving the strategic plan. This ensures that the plan is actually shaping the activities of the institution, and isn't simply living in a file somewhere until there's a need for a new one.

These performance indicators also show whether the strategic plan is working. When these measures aren't being met, the organization isn't necessarily doing anything wrong. The strategic plan might not meet the needs of the institution any longer. If the goal is to promote information-literate citizens, and the measure is to fund twenty information literacy programs each year, but no one is attending these programs and the community is not interested in them, perhaps the strategic plan doesn't work for the library that made it. Maybe the funding has not been enough to provide twenty worthwhile information literacy activities, because other priorities have taken precedence. Whatever the reason, when these indicators aren't met, it might be time to revise the strategic plan, even after only a year or two. This should be done thoughtfully, of course, to ensure that the next iteration of this living document better captures the library's goals.

## Step 6: Allowing Review and Input

Once the imperatives, objectives, strategies, and performance indicators are identified, the document is written and disseminated to all of the stakeholders impacted. Again, focus groups or surveys may be a good way to solicit input. Focus groups are especially valuable for stakeholders such as patrons, whose input is extremely valuable but who can't or won't all read the finished product. Conversations with stakeholders about the strategic plan can be a good way to approach this stage of input, since people can ask questions and clarify points better in person. Ideas should be integrated into the final document whenever possible. Though not all feedback is relevant, stakeholders are more willing to buy in when they know their thoughts matter.

## Step 7: Implementing the Plan

The final stage of the strategic plan is implementation. This is the "doing" phase where the concrete actions identified actually occur. As mentioned above, throughout this phase the ongoing assessment of the performance indicators is helpful to guide further revisions and changes. After all, as discussed in chapter 1, sometimes a plan turns out to be useless once it reaches the implementation phase.

# ◎ Strategic Planning for Units

Though this process is quite formalized as described above, for a smaller unit of a library, strategic planning does not need to be this complicated or involved. It can consist of long-term goal setting and assessment planning. For most libraries, except for maybe the biggest research libraries, each individual department does not need a fully formulated strategic plan. This is overkill, and might waste time better spent doing something else. Long-term goals and an intentional, deliberative plan for assessment purposes are absolutely necessary, but a full, formal planning process is not. When doing this goal setting, it is useful to start with one's own long-term goals for the unit, and then expand to the goals of staff and frequent patrons.

Also talk to the library director, since the unit's strategic goals need to align with and support the library's larger objectives as well as the strategic aims of the institution. This is important because, as mentioned above, resources are allocated in part based on the larger strategic plan. This is also significant because these goals are the major long-term objectives of the organization—it makes good sense from a management perspective to align with them.

When planning, think about goals as outcomes. For instance, a desired outcome might be to ensure that students have timely access to library instruction. Next, ask why this outcome is important. Again, good outcomes often align with university or library strategic goals. Outcomes might also target a particular requirement for accreditation. In this case, timely access to library instruction aligns with a Southern Association of Colleges and Schools Commission on Colleges (SACSCOC) accreditation requirement for academic libraries. At a public library, an outcome might be to have two books for every one potential patron, in order to fulfill a state requirement. Whatever the outcome is, have a clear sense of why it was chosen. What does it achieve? Where does it move the unit?

Also consider what activities would potentially contribute to achieving the goal. For instance, to improve student access to library collections, what could the library implement that would actually lead to this improvement? If there is no actionable way to reach the goal, then there is no point in measuring it. The whole idea of this exercise is to improve what the unit does by making changes or implementing new services or projects to achieve an end.

Also make sure the goal is realistic, given the current situation and the expectations for the near to middle term. For instance, a goal might be to process a large archival collection in a short amount of time, but if the funding doesn't exist to get staff resources to achieve this goal, and securing the funding is unlikely, this is not a good objective. There's a significant likelihood that the unit won't achieve it. This is not to discourage the setting of stretch goals. These are extremely handy because they can push staff to strive for a better quality of service than was provided in the past. However, there is a big difference between stretch goals and fantasy goals, and managers need to recognize when the line is crossed from one to the other.

Consider the wording of outcomes carefully. The wording can be reasonably simple, but it has to be actionable. One common, helpful suggestion is that outcomes, like the objectives on which they're based, should be a verb, an adjective, and a noun. For instance, an outcome might be to "increase customer satisfaction," or "increase student information literacy." This is a good way to start, though adding a little bit more detail can clarify things. That said, don't add too much more, because overly elaborate outcomes become difficult to measure. A more descriptive outcome might be something like, "increase patron access to needed library services." Again, whatever way an outcome is conveyed, make sure it's actionable, achievable, challenging, and easy enough to measure.

Finally, when goal setting, remember that mid-term and long-term strategic goals aren't simply any old thing the unit needs to get done. These goals need to represent the most important concerns: key areas where expanding and improving are required to stay vital and fulfill the unit's purpose. Don't just check a box to show the staff has done a list of things—this needs to be goal setting to get the unit from one stage of development to the next.

## Strategic Planning for Libraries and Organizations

In addition to the strategic planning for a single unit, middle managers are often involved in strategic planning for the library as a whole. They are in a position of authority that almost certainly gives them a seat at the table to make the big decisions that guide the library's future development. Strategic planning for the library is not very different than for a unit, though the picture is bigger. The process for library strategic planning is also likely to be much more structured, and follow closely steps similar to those described earlier in this chapter.

If simply participating in the strategic planning process, do so in good faith. Remember that, as a member of the strategic planning group, a middle manager represents the interests of their unit, and having measures related to this unit in the strategic plan is going to help get resources later on, since they are frequently allocated based on priorities in the strategic plan. This does not mean that managers should be obnoxious about getting all priorities listed in the plan, even those that may not fit well or are not important to the rest of the group. It does mean that managers shouldn't let their biggest priorities get left out. Know how the unit fits into the larger picture—represent that to the group doing strategic planning. This is especially true when serving on behalf of the library in a strategic planning process for the entire city, county, school, or university.

If leading the strategic planning effort for the library, or for the larger institution, the most important job is making sure everyone who needs to be heard is heard. The best way to achieve this is to have a strong, structured process that provides plenty of opportunities for a diverse array of stakeholders to be involved. That said, the best strategic planning processes are usually carried out by one or two people, or maybe a very small group of committed individuals, working diligently to create a plan based on a wide array of feedback. If the core strategic planning group is too large, the plan will not be written in a timely or streamlined fashion. This is a difficult balancing act because, on the one hand, the majority of the work requires a very small number of people doing a lot and, on the other hand, meaningful input from many people should shape the end product. Having the right people in the main group is essential. The people who ultimately work on the plan need to take input graciously, and incorporate it well, even when they are the primary architects of what is written. The first part of this book about project management might be helpful if leading this kind of effort, as it is exactly the type of project that builds management capabilities.

All of this should make clear one very important point: if asked to participate in a strategic planning process, say yes! This process has a huge impact on who gets resources, what projects get the most attention, and the path the organization takes for many years.

## ⊚ Assessment Plans

Related to strategic planning, many organizations require a formal, annual assessment plan for each department based on outcomes and objectives. For institutions of higher education, this is required for many reasons, but especially because of accreditation, which requires each major unit of the institution to show that it participates in a continuous improvement process. For cities and other government agencies, this might be done for funding or other reporting. Whatever the reason, and even if it isn't required, a regular continuous improvement process is essential to good management. Even individual employees get annual evaluations to help them improve. Why wouldn't the library undergo the same kind of evaluation? Think of these annual assessment plans as a formalized and intentional process that focuses on improving the organization by analyzing the most meaningful data collected across a year. Libraries are full of data that tracks all kinds of things. The assessment plan is the method used to figure out what data is meaningful, and what it means.

An assessment plan is an annual measure of whether a unit has achieved its objectives. It should list the outcomes discussed earlier, and the performance indicators used to assess the extent to which these are achieved. Performance indicators, or measures, should be clearly worded and targeted. Many people make them way too broad, such that they aren't measurable. In contrast to outcomes, which are sometimes quite simple, measures are direct. For instance, let's consider "increase customer satisfaction" as the outcome. This is fairly vague. To measure this outcome, one might say "increase user ratings for question 3, related to customer satisfaction with access services, on our annual user satisfaction survey." This is much more targeted and it is also measurable. An even better goal might be "increase user ratings every year by at least 5 percentage points on question 3, related to user satisfaction with access services, on our annual user satisfaction survey." This is even clearer about the goal, but when does the unit stop increasing this satisfaction measure? What happens if they hit a ceiling? An even better wording would be "increase user ratings every year by at least 5 percentage points on question 3, related to user satisfaction with access services, on our annual user satisfaction survey, until our rating is 90 percent satisfaction." This explains how much the unit hopes to raise satisfaction annually, and also when it will no longer need to strive to improve this measure. This is really well worded.

When choosing data to include in an assessment plan, keep it simple. Target the most meaningful information. If there are too many data points, the real core of the assessment is buried. Remember when picking data that this isn't simply a required report—it is something that can help leadership make the best decisions about the future of the unit.

Think about capturing both direct and indirect data for each outcome. Another way to view this is "what is happening," and "what do people think about what is happening." For direct data, one might choose usage statistics for electronic journals and for indirect, satisfaction survey results related to electronic journal holdings. In other words, how are people using the journals? What do people think about the journals? Those are different directions from which to look at the same thing, and they both give essential, meaningful data.

Once outcomes and measures are identified, the next step is to collect data periodically, usually every year, and to use that data to determine how well outcomes are achieved. Don't simply gather data, present it, and say the unit did or did not achieve what it hoped to. Analyze it, explain why it turned out the way it did—what worked and what didn't—and make an action plan to continue to improve in areas where the unit fell short. A really good assessment plan also identifies what resources are needed to improve in future years, and the people in the unit who are responsible for making sure that those improvements are happening. Again, if the outcomes and measures are easily mapped to the library and university strategic plans, this makes asking for the resources needed even easier.

Remember, this is a meaningful process, or at least, it should be. There is no point to doing assessment that isn't going to help make better decisions. As the unit heads, middle managers decide whether they are going to buy into the process, and how much effort they put in to make it meaningful. The easiest solution might be to do the bare minimum, but why not make it something that helps in the long run?

Ultimately, assessment and strategic planning, like most other things related to management, are not exact sciences. If strategy is simply a pattern in a string of decisions, and planning is more useful as a way of thinking through all of the potential contingencies, then strategic planning is simply a way to bring order to the decision-making of a leader or leadership group, based on a reasoned and thoughtful review of all of the possible contingencies. This creates an intentional approach to decision-making, with the aim of reaching well-defined objectives. Obviously, these goals can change over time. Perhaps a new opportunity becomes available that completely changes the priorities, or a crisis occurs, like a wildfire or a hurricane, that shifts the leadership's focus. Strong leaders know how to stick to the plan, and know when to alter it in recognition of new realities.

## Key Points

- Strategy is a pattern of decision-making.
- Strategic planning is a way of bringing order to leadership's decision-making.
- Strategic planning is a multi-step process that identifies objectives.
- Units, libraries, and institutions can all participate in strategic planning activities, even if not every such activity leads to a formalized strategic plan.
- Assessment plans are the way the library measures its performance on an annual basis. These are related to, but distinct from, strategic plans.

## References

Mintzberg, Henry. 1978. "Patterns in Strategy Formation." *Management Science* 24 (9): 934–48. JSTOR.

# CHAPTER 11

# Promoting and Transforming Organizational Culture

ONE OF THE MOST FAMOUS EXAMPLES of a company with a strong organizational culture comes from an industry that might be surprising, since it has received a lot of criticism for poor customer service and work conditions. This is, of course, the U.S. airline industry, and the company is Southwest Airlines. Known for providing excellent customer service, including flexibility in rescheduling flights, Southwest inspires a cult following among customers, many of whom pay a premium to fly Southwest. The leadership of Southwest maintains that part of the reason for this excellent customer service is the strong organizational culture at the company (Parker 2008). Southwest operates with the belief that if employees are treated well, then they, in turn, treat customers well, and customers return again and again.

Following the terrorist attacks on September 11, 2001, Southwest went against industry norms and, in alignment with these guiding principles, allowed all customers to receive refunds on flights. They also chose not to let employees go, despite the financial struggles of the airline industry. These decisions impacted their stock for a time, but Southwest was able to rebound with greater customer loyalty and employee devotion. The leadership made risky decisions that hurt the company's bottom line, but strengthened their market position in the long run (Parker 2008). This is why organizational culture is important. Culture drives the employee experience and, ultimately, the patron experience. A great organizational culture is a rare and valuable thing, and a poor one is a problem that takes a lot of time and effort to fix.

Middle managers are in a particularly precarious position when it comes to creating and maintaining the organizational culture of an institution. On the one hand, at this level, managers are unlikely to be in control of the overall culture. Usually, this is a top-down facet of the workplace that comes from the executive levels. On the other hand, middle managers are directly responsible for promoting and perpetuating the organizational culture in their individual units, and sometimes for transforming them. Managers who significantly diverge from the prevailing management style in the organization are bound to have a difficult time. Still, middle managers do hold a lot of agency when it comes to culture. They can identify the best values and behaviors of their institution and focus on promoting those, rather than the less desirable ones. As Edgar H. Schein and Peter A. Schein say in *Organizational Culture and Leadership*, "leadership is the management of culture" (2016, 125). Dealing with the organization's culture is one of the key roles of any manager.

## Definitions

Organizational culture: The values and behaviors that shape the social and psychological ethos of a workplace.

Values: Principles and standards of behavior.

## ⊚ What Is Organizational Culture?

At its most basic level, an organization's culture can be defined as the values and behaviors that shape the social and psychological ethos of a workplace—in other words, the aspects of an institution that are prized and promoted by those that work there. These values and behaviors should be easy to identify, even for the most entry-level employee. They ought to be the core of value statements, missions, and other strategic planning documents, and an institution's practices should align with these.

For instance, an organization that values integrity in its core values would probably put a lot of stress on the importance of ethics for its employees. An organization that values sustainability would have programs to encourage energy-efficient work spaces and recycling. Often missions have geographic regions—either local, national, or international—which determine a lot about how an organization envisions its reach, allocates resources, and focuses its efforts. Remember that the top-level values, goals, and mission of an organization should mirror the priorities of those at the highest level of leadership.

Many of the strongest organizations have the strongest cultures. Think of major Fortune 500 companies that are famous for employee and customer satisfaction, such as Southwest mentioned earlier, or Google. Their success is determined in part by a culture that they promote at all levels, in the way people behave and decisions are made. For Southwest, this is embodied through customer- and employee-focused policies. At Google, it manifests as a work culture for software developers that supports innovation, entrepreneurship, and engineering excellence by allowing programmers to work on whatever projects interest them for a portion of their allocated work hours. Even Amazon, not always known as an easy environment for employees, is recognized for being customer focused to the exclusion of almost any other concern, which the company calls "customer obsession." Though Southwest and Amazon approach customer service, and what leads to good customer service, differently, they both have unique cultures that ultimately result in similar ends.

Elements of organizational culture include how the organization views and relates to its community, patrons, employees, and other stakeholders, and especially the behavior of leaders; how the organization expects these constituents to interact with and treat one another; how effectiveness is defined by the organization; and the emotions and feelings that are acceptable and unacceptable to express in social settings (Schein and Schein 2016). At the core of all these elements are communication and social interaction. Organizational culture is strongly associated with the way people are treated by and within the workplace.

One example of this might be how customer service is handled at a library. Most libraries are, in varying degrees, customer focused. The way this focus is implemented at individual libraries has a significant impact on the morale and outlook of the staff. If the employees feel like "the customer is always right" even when the customer is wrong, and therefore believe that management does not support their decisions when those conclusions are contrary to the wishes of patrons, this can cause a staff morale issue because staff won't feel like they have the authority to enforce the policies of the library. If the leadership always sides with employees, and never listens to customers, the organization has the opposite problem—employees who are emboldened, but maybe aren't behaving in the best interests of the patrons, or who even feel antagonistic toward patrons. As these examples show, the organizational culture of a library—or the way that different groups of people are expected to interact and the behavior of leadership—has a significant impact on many aspects of an institution.

Other elements that contribute to the organization's culture include how hierarchical it is, the rapidity with which decisions and changes occur, the relation of people to tasks in decision-making, the main functional areas, and the subcultures throughout a workplace (Schein and Schein 2016). Different types of employees work well in different types of settings. Some people prefer a less hierarchical structure, where they feel emboldened to talk between levels of authority as needed, and others need the structure that comes from a greater degree of hierarchy. A manager who comes in and tries to institute a hierarchical structure in a workplace that has not traditionally had a strict hierarchy will have a difficult time doing so. In libraries, many employees are resistant to change, especially when they have performed the same task in the same way for many years. A library where processes and policies frequently change would not be a good fit for these types of people. As this example shows, understanding the existing organizational culture is important, especially before any changes can be made. Misreading the culture can lead to many easy-to-avoid mistakes on the part of a new manager. Schein and Schein include an excellent discussion of what makes an organization's culture for those interested in the topic (2016).

## ⊚ Types of Organizational Cultures

To understand the existing organizational culture, managers must first identify the type of culture at their workplace. In 1981, Robert Quinn and John Rohrbaugh developed what is called the Competing Values Framework. This framework measures the values of an organization related to two dimensions of the organizational culture: the internal-external dimension and the stability-flexibility dimension. According to their research, an organization's values, measured by these dimensions, are indicative of the type of organizational culture. Though all organizations need to be, to some degree, both internally and externally focused, as well as have some stability and some flexibility, most organizations value one side over the other.

Where an institution falls on the internal-external dimension indicates whether it is focused mostly on internal collaborations, development, and coordination, or external competitors, markets, and innovations, in order to grow. The stability-flexibility dimension indicates whether an institution focuses on developing reliability through set procedures, budgets, and planning, or through flexible structures and a focus on individuals and activities. Where an organization falls on the axis between each set of values determines the type of organizational culture.

The four types of organizational cultures, based on these dimensions and defined in Kim S. Cameron and Robert E. Quinn's *Diagnosing and Changing Organizational Culture* (2011), are:

- Adhocracy: Externally focused and flexible, this is a dynamic organizational culture that values creating and entrepreneurship. People are encouraged to experiment thoughtfully. Change is often rapid and transformational. A new library that is expanding fast in directions that are cutting edge would likely be an adhocracy.
- Clan: Internally focused and flexible, these are collaborative organizations that often feel like families. Change takes a long time, because tradition and loyalty are valued. Cohesion and employee engagement is important. These organizations are very friendly and people focused. Libraries where colleagues are socially close, with a strong, devoted following from patrons, would be a clan. Many local and small academic libraries are clans, with a focus on interpersonal relationships and everyday kindnesses.
- Hierarchy: Internally focused and stable, in hierarchical cultures, efficiency and smooth operations of the organization are highly prized. This is a formalized workplace with clear procedures and guidelines, and a focus on avoiding errors. Caution in decision-making is common, and so change happens in small ways over time. The librarians in *Desk Set*, a 1957 movie starring Katherine Hepburn and Spencer Tracy, have a hierarchical organizational culture. In the film, Hepburn's character runs a reference library associated with a media company. Her focus is on answering questions as quickly and correctly as possible. She is fighting to keep a computer from taking over many of her responsibilities, a role with which many modern-day librarians can sympathize.
- Market: Externally focused and stable, these organizations value getting a lot done and reaching aggressive goals. Change is rapid and in response to the needs of customers. Competition drives this organizational culture. Libraries don't tend to be market driven, though many of the larger organizations that contain libraries might be, such as universities, corporations, or hospital systems. A special librarian at a multinational corporation is likely to feel the pressure to reach ever more difficult goals with fewer resources if the institution has a market culture.

Understanding each type of organization is important, because some people work better in specific settings. As previously mentioned, when employees seem displeased with a work environment, it is often because they don't fit in with the culture. For instance, an employee might be in a clan type of organization, but may not enjoy socializing with colleagues. This person might do well in a hierarchical structure, where the focus is on efficiency and smooth operations rather than collaboration. Conversely, someone who values collaboration would likely do poorly in a market type of organization, where competition often drives growth rather than everyone working together.

Middle managers in particular should know the type of organization they favor, as well as the type of organization in which they are working, because it can have such a significant impact on fellow employees. A manager that favors the adhocracy type of organizational culture probably manages with those values at the forefront. This impacts that person's management style, and in turn, the employees. In addition, if the culture of the larger organization contrasts with an individual manager's style, it may cause problems. For this reason, middle managers may have to adjust to fit with the larger culture.

Finally, remember that how well employees fit into an organization may be impacted by their culture of origin. Many cultures view work, the appropriate way to interact at work, and the best way to organize an institution differently. While organizational cultures such as the clan model are friendly and welcoming for those who share the same values and background, they might also exclude people without the same cultural experiences. Similarly, while the flexibility and lack of rigid structure in the adhocracy might give some employees a sense of self-determination, they may also appear disrespectful to others. Middle managers must be prepared to make sure the culture doesn't exclude employees with different values.

## Identifying an Organization's Culture

The culture of an organization may not present itself immediately, or may not align with the stated values, goals, or mission of that organization. A library's stated values may prize sustainability, but in practice, there are no actual steps taken toward this end. Hiring managers might talk about how fun it is to work at a library when in reality, every day just drags on, or worse, turnover is high and employee satisfaction is low. For this reason, it is important to pay attention to the reality on the ground, not just the stated intentions.

There are many different indicators that point to the true organizational culture. Beyond the strategic goals and mission mentioned above, organizational charts, public budgets, and human resource policies are good indicators. Budgets are important because money is often the scarcest resource in any organization. An institution values most the departments it funds best. If a university claims that the library is the heart of their operation, but the library's funding is miniscule, its stated values are not indicative of what is really important.

Organizational charts, like budgets, also show what is esteemed by an organization. Relevant to the library, one of the most important indicators of how it is viewed is the level at which the library director reports. At an institution of higher education, for instance, a library director often reports to the provost. If the library director doesn't report at this level, it might indicate a lack of concern on the part of the provost for the well-being of the library. A library reporting directly to the chief information officer, instead of to a library director, is also an important clue about the role of the library at that institution. Though this arrangement can work really well at some places where the CIO has respect for the value of libraries, it can also function poorly, especially if the CIO has sold this arrangement to the upper administration as a cost-saving measure. Often, this results in a CIO who is reallocating funding away from the library and toward other IT needs. This arrangement is especially common in school districts, but occasionally appears in city governments and institutions of higher education. Whatever the success of the arrangement, a library that reports to a CIO indicates the aspects of the library's operation an institution values most, namely the virtual services. As these examples show, where a library reports in the organizational structure says a lot about how it is viewed, why it is valued and, sometimes, *if* it is valued.

Organizational charts also indicate how hierarchical that organization is. Some libraries have fairly flat organizational structures where everyone reports to the director, and some have deep organizational structures where authority is vested in different pockets throughout the staff. Some people work better with a flat management structure, because they feel that they can work directly with the director. Some work better with a hierarchical structure where there is a clear middle manager in charge of their area, to whom they can go whenever they need assistance.

There are pros and cons to both types of organizational structures. The flat structure gives individual employees more autonomy, as well as direct interaction with the top-level administrator at all times, and ensures the director has vested power to supervise every employee and all library operations. These structures are often taxing for directors because they require supervision of so many employees at once, and often individual employees don't get the same level of support and mentorship they might get with a more focused manager. Also, while some directors are able to manage this type of structure really well to promote egalitarianism and collaboration among all staff, some employ it to assert control, and might micromanage staff.

A more layered organizational structure removes lower-level library employees from regular, direct interaction with the top-level administrators, making the potential much higher for those employees to feel disregarded. The benefit of this structure is that middle managers with clear specialization in the areas they supervise are able to manage the day-to-day operations in an area, and can work one on one with those employees to help them develop and grow in their positions. While a hierarchical structure may immediately seem more limiting for employees, this depends on how the structure is implemented and how it is managed. For administrators, this style often frees up time by requiring supervision of just a subset of middle managers. This allows a focus on professional development for more senior employees. Notably, this structure inevitably removes directors from the day-to-day operations in certain areas of the library, which can lead to problems that go undiscovered or ignored. This is all to say that, no matter what the organizational structure, the structure at a library reveals a lot about the culture.

The organizational structure also provides a lot of indicators about the context in which the library operates. A relatively small city government where the library is only one of a few units is probably more flexible and less rigid than a library in a major metropolitan area where there are lots of city employees and levels of management between lower-level staff and the top library administrator. For academic librarians, the experience at an institution that is a member of a large university system varies greatly from one at a small, private liberal arts college. Where there might be greater stability and more structure in a university system, there are also many rules and layers of approval that are not present at a private college that isn't a part of state government. Working for any library that is funded by taxes is necessarily more restrictive than a private institution, since there is a greater degree of accountability required when acting as a steward of public funds.

The human resource policies of an institution also reveal a lot about the culture. For instance, an organization that purports to be casual, flexible, and accommodating toward staff, but has a strict dress code and rigid requirements for when employees take lunches, might not be as employee friendly as claimed. On the other hand, an institution that asserts the safety and well-being of their employees and patrons as its highest priority, and has an active employee wellness program and a host of safety guidelines and procedures, likely lives its values.

Beyond the budget, structure, and policies of an institution, there are other indicators that might reveal the culture. Are employees working late every night? What kind of social activities do they participate in? How are groups of people involved in decision-making, and who are these groups of people? How is feedback given? Many of these questions can be answered by talking to fellow employees to find out about the situation on the ground. There may also be relevant data available from Human Resources. For instance, an institution might participate in the *Chronicle of Higher Education*'s Great Colleges to Work For annual culture survey or another, similar measure available to governments or in K–12 educational settings.

Finally, listening to the top-level administrators in an organization, and watching how they act, is the biggest clue to the organization's culture because it is set from the top down. If the library director repeatedly says that work-life balance is important, but the director and the managers stay until 9:00 p.m. every day, those statements may not accurately align with reality. Similarly, if a director says that he or she values a culture of openness and mutual respect, but does not treat fellow employees well and frequently punishes them for voicing dissenting opinions, employees are going to feel as though they risk their jobs if they speak up. On the other hand, a director who says that work output and efficiency at all costs is critical, but is very flexible and accommodating with employees, might indicate that the culture is not as rigid as it purports to be.

No matter what the situation, it is important to remember that the stated values of an institution might not match the actual organizational culture. Especially in the early days of working at a new library, or when considering working for a new library, remember to pay attention to the indicators mentioned above to get an idea of what the reality is.

## ◎ Transforming Organizational Culture

Once managers have identified an institution's culture, they can determine whether or not the culture needs to be changed. Many, many reams of paper have been spent discussing how to transform an organizational culture, including a few of the books cited in this chapter. This is often one of the most difficult tasks put in front of a new manager. Though transforming a library's culture often falls to a director, middle managers are necessarily involved in this process. As a result, this section of the chapter covers the higher-level changes involved even though they might not be the exclusive purview of middle management. For a more in-depth discussion of organizational change in libraries, Lisa K. Hussey and Diane L. Velasquez's *Library Management 101* (2019) provides excellent coverage of this topic.

Note that changes to organizational culture cannot simply flow from an organization's leaders down to the rest of their staff. They must be driven and implemented from the bottom up. In other words, a manager who comes in and issues a lot of orders about what the culture should be, without doing the hard work of engaging all levels of employees and stakeholders in the process, is almost certain to fail. This is not something that an edict can fix. It must be a participatory process. As discussed in chapter 3 about group formation, any process that involves a group of employees making significant decisions about the way a library operates is going to result in a degree of conflict. People will feel left out, will be upset that what is implemented does not meet their expectations, and may lash out because of it. Moreover, some employees are perfectly happy with the current state of things, and won't want to change.

For these reasons, though no process suits every library in every situation, leaders probably want to create a working group or other team when large-scale changes to organizational culture are required. This group must always include different types of employees, both professional and paraprofessional, with the highest possible equality of opinion and responsibility in the context of the team. This process might include everyone in a small unit, but for larger units, there should be plenty of opportunities for input from each member of the staff. If the library is due for a revision to its strategic plan and values, discussed in chapter 10, then this goes hand in hand with that process, particularly the SWOT analysis, which may provide opportunities for participation and input.

The manager, or an entire library, might also choose to do an annual survey of employees specifically focused on staff satisfaction, work culture, and unit operations. On this survey, trends are important, as well as outliers and departures from trends. For instance, a manager may find that while most of the library staff answers positively for most of the questions, staff consistently reports that there are not enough employees to achieve goals. This trend might indicate that employees are feeling overworked and that there might be an issue with work-life balance. Conversely, most employees might rate the unit well for diversity, but there are one or two outliers. This may suggest that diversity measures are missing a group of employees who are not feeling represented. Instituting such a survey might be a good first step in a unit that does not yet seem ready for change, as it can help build a case for it and might also shed light on why certain employees are resisting it.

## Reviewing the Mission and Values

As mentioned above, reviewing the mission and values of an organization goes hand in hand with culture change. If the organization's activities are not lining up with the mission and values, it may mean that the activities of the organization need to be realigned. It is also possible that the mission needs to be reviewed and revised based on the changes the organization has undergone. As mentioned elsewhere, people tend to view the mission and values as immutable features of a unit, but they can and should change as needed.

Changing a mission and values makes the most sense when the cultural problem is directly related to the mismatch with the stated values and mission—in other words, when the mission and values are outdated, forcing the library or library units into certain modes of operation that either highlight or ignore important factors of the current operations. For instance, a mission for a public library might require revisions if the makeup of a surrounding community has changed substantially since the mission was originally written. A mission for a public library in a community that has become much more diverse since the last revision to the mission, and that doesn't appropriately recognize this diversity, is out of date. On the other hand, changing a mission when the cultural problem stems from something other than a mismatched mission, such as HR procedures or the top-down communication approach of the executive leadership, doesn't always make a lot of sense.

That said, changes to the mission and values, done at the same time as a library is working through other alterations to the work culture, can be an important way of signaling the new direction for the organization. These also go hand in hand as the activities involved in strategic planning, such as SWOT analysis, are related to the strengths and weaknesses of the library, including culture issues.

## Revising the Organizational Structure

The structure of a library is fundamentally linked to the culture of the organization. This determines the distribution of power throughout the library, as discussed earlier. The structure of the library determines the level of authority different employees and groups of employees have and who reports directly to the executive leadership. Reporting to the library director is an important signal of power, because these people have the most visibility and the most direct line of communication with the person who ultimate makes many of the high-priority decisions. When looking at structure, the first consideration should be who ought to report to the director.

The size of individual units within an organization's structure also expresses the values and culture of the institution. For instance, a library with a large contingent of electronic resource–related librarians probably puts a high priority on virtual services. Librarians who are not excited to work with e-resources are not a good fit in that culture. This institution might also be innovative or cutting edge. However, a library mostly made up of public services librarians obviously puts a big premium on "high-touch" services and may not spend as much time on technical services–related issues. A cataloger might not feel very valued at this institution, as the primary focus is not likely to be that aspect of library operations.

Many times, managers inherit organizational structures that are outdated or that don't fit with their vision. Part of the job, in these cases, is reorganizing positions so that the resources are dedicated to areas of highest priority. Managers contemplating a reorganization should remember that they are telegraphing to their employees what they value, not lines of reporting.

## Aligning Policies and Protocols

Once the mission and values have changed, the library has to align policies and procedures with these new organizational priorities. If the library claims to support work-life balance, for instance, then policies should align with that value. In other words, policies might stipulate that emails shouldn't be sent after 6:00 p.m., work-from-home opportunities should be made available when possible, and flexible start and stop times could be approved.

All library policies should be reviewed, even some that seem unrelated to organizational culture. In circulation, for instance, policies related to overdue fines might be rewritten if such fines are proving to be overly burdensome for low-income patrons, especially in libraries where providing access to print resources is of particular value. In a library focused on access, technical services protocols related to buying technology might also contribute to the overall culture, since the type of technology purchased might not be accessible to many patrons who are not tech-savvy, or who lack a home connection to the internet.

When reviewing the general activities of the library, protocols should include both formal and informal activities. Sometimes, the informal ways that staff act toward one another or toward patrons can have a huge impact on the overall culture of a library. Often, these are not written ways of being. Rather, they are the established modes of communication that are passed on from one employee to another. One could consider these interactions similar to the common fight couples have—where one person gets mad, not because of what the partner has said, but because of how it was said. These informal ways of interacting are often a matter of how things are communicated, the types of traditions a library's staff may pass on, or the nonverbal cues that are shared and understood among employees.

Remember that sometimes, even generally positive traditions and activities might unintentionally exclude members of the staff. For example, a library might have an annual staff picnic at a gazebo in a state park. If a staff member in a wheelchair is hired, and this gazebo is not accessible, then suddenly this tradition might contribute to a culture that isn't welcoming of certain groups of people. Not every tradition that excludes staff members is so obvious, so it's important to look out for such issues.

## Creating Accountability

The last, but perhaps the most important, element in creating a new organizational culture at a library or in a unit is the establishment of accountability. Accountability starts with the management team, including middle managers. In order for the culture to change, the managers must hold themselves to the standards of behavior expected from everyone else. If the rule is to send emails before 6:00 p.m., then that should start with the management team. If sustainability is a value in the library, the managers must be seen engaging in recycling. They must also ensure that those who don't meet these standards are mentored and coached until they are able to contribute to the overall culture of the organization.

Though culture may seem like an intangible aspect of library leadership compared to many more direct concerns, such as how to fund the library for another year, a bad culture runs the risk of sinking everything else a library is trying to achieve. Anyone who has worked in such a bad culture or, even worse, a good culture that suddenly turned bad with the arrival of a new director, can attest to the significant impediment that the crash in morale, motivation, and quality brings.

## 🌀 Key Points

- Organizational culture is one of the most significant factors that determine success in a professional setting.
- Though middle managers may not have control over the culture of the larger organization, they can set the culture in their own unit.
- Identifying the type of culture the unit has at present, and whether or not the organization's stated values align with policies and practices, is the first step toward understanding culture.
- When a library's culture is dysfunctional, it needs to be transformed.
- To change a library's culture, leaders must review the mission, policies, and structure of the library, and then hold library staff accountable for following these revised documents.

## 🌀 References

Cameron, Kim S., and Robert E. Quinn. 2011. *Diagnosing and Changing Organizational Culture: Based on the Competing Values Framework*, 3rd edition. San Francisco: Jossey-Bassey. Kindle.

Hussey, Lisa K., and Diane L. Velasquez, eds. 2019. *Library Management 101: A Practical Guide*. Chicago: ALA Editions. Kindle.

Parker, James F. 2008. *Do the Right Thing: How Dedicated Employees Create Loyal Customers and Large Profits*. Upper Saddle River, NJ: Prentice Hall. Kindle.

Quinn, Robert E., and John Rohrbaugh. 1981. "The Competing Values Approach to Organizational Culture." *Public Productivity Review* 5 (2): 122–40. JSTOR.

Schein, Edgar H., and Peter A. Schein. 2016. *Organizational Culture and Leadership*. Hoboken, NJ: Wiley. EBSCO eBook Collection.

# CHAPTER 12

# Developing Professionally through Middle Management

SUCCESS AS A MIDDLE MANAGER DOES NOT necessarily translate to success in upper administration, but there are key skills gained in middle management that can help those who aspire to the highest levels of library administration. The most important include the ability to take responsibility for the operations of a unit, to manage people and resources, and to support the mission of the institution. As a middle manager, there are also many opportunities to step out of the library by serving on significant committees across city government or the university, where a librarian can begin to learn the outward-facing role of a director. Having experience in each of these areas, and being able to discuss these experiences in thoughtful and insightful ways, goes a long way toward securing that first job as a head librarian.

Remember that, when an institution is interviewing for a library director, it is looking for someone who can be the chief library officer in the organization. Directors must be the go-to librarians, as they are probably the highest ranking on staff. They are trusted to keep the library functioning with little input from those higher up who lack professional training as librarians. The institution needs somebody who can stand on his or her own two feet, in this regard. The library is also looking for candidates who understand the larger context: a public librarian who knows city government, or an academic librarian who understands how academic affairs and universities work. This includes knowing how the institution is funded, what laws impact operations, and how the library fits into the bigger picture. Library directors also spend a lot of time working with other units across an organization, rather than just the staff of the library itself, and must have some understanding of what those units do and why they are important. As a result, a candidate for a director position has to have many, varied competencies before ever getting hired, either through direct experience or observed insight.

Supervising the day-to-day operations of a unit is one important aspect of middle management, discussed throughout this second part of the book, that can help managers grow into directors. This experience impacts three main professional competencies: exercising professional judgement, allocating resources, and mentoring and coordinating others.

Middle managers have countless opportunities to exercise their professional judgement on a daily basis. For one, middle managers learn from dealing with the small everyday crises, which are stepping stones toward the many big crises that administrators have to navigate. For example, as a head of public services, one might be asked to deal with a patron who has become belligerent. Dealing with this patron teaches managers how to deal with quarrelsome donors or faculty members in high-stakes situations as an administrator. For a head of tech services, software might get hacked, exposing patron data. Though an unfortunate situation, this demonstrates concretely what to look for in software licensing in the future as the administrator asked to sign on the dotted line. Going through budget cuts as the head of a unit models the way cuts can be weathered when in charge of a whole library. Pay attention to these little crises, because they are the training ground for those seeking further responsibility. They develop the leadership muscles needed to have sound professional judgment, and to convey this judgement through concrete examples to potential employers.

Mentoring and coordinating employees as a middle manager is also extremely valuable for a future director. Today's small squabbles between a reference librarian and circulation clerk predict the interdepartmental issues that make a director dream of retirement tomorrow. This is also extremely valuable when it comes to eventually managing managers. As a manager of managers, one needs to be able to mentor librarians who are themselves actively mentoring others. These are not early-career librarians, though they may be new middle managers. Mentoring mentors is, at times, an odd Texas two-step. It requires thinking about the manager, and how that manager operates and impacts the professional development of an employee, whose happiness and professional development is also the ultimate responsibility of the director. Becoming a great mentor in the relatively less complex setting of manager to single practitioner will prepare a librarian to mentor other managers, by providing opportunities to meaningfully reflect on what works and what doesn't. The insights gained through such reflection are extremely valuable when working with new managers, who can benefit from these insights and possibly avoid the same mistakes.

Finally, though budgeting is often a key activity of an administrator, allocating resources is really the domain of middle managers. Managers of units are often primarily responsible for determining what resources are assigned to different services and activities, and where the focus is for the unit, especially as it relates to the library's mission and goals. Many of the important decisions that administrators make are exactly these, though on a larger scale. Becoming familiar with how to allocate these resources is key to moving into upper administration. Furthermore, the more managers understand and participate in the budgeting process, the better prepared they are when it is their turn to lead it. Middle managers have a unique chance to work with the director and find out where money is coming from, where it is going, and what rules exist about how it is spent. This is administrator 101!

As mentioned above, there are also opportunities as a middle manager to work with other departments across the city, or to participate in university-wide initiatives, as well as occasions to meet with community stakeholders, vendors, and donors, that might not have been available in previous roles. The visibility of a middle manager, especially at the assistant director or dean level, can open many doors. Take these opportunities. A director is the library's CEO, the representative in the organization and the community. Take every chance offered to get this experience, because it's essential and can be hard to come by.

One last note: a middle manager's supervisor is often the director. Learn from the director, and really pay attention to how he or she handles every situation, even those that seem straightforward. The nuances of leading a library are much clearer when working more closely with the director than in previous roles. Watching and asking questions about how a director handles a challenge like a budget cut or a staff conflict can provide insight into how the approach worked, and what could have been handled differently. Even a bad decision by the director provides an opportunity to observe how the mistake was made and to determine how it could have been avoided, as well as a chance to see how the director recovers from it. Don't be afraid to ask administrators why they did what they did, and how they would have handled it differently, knowing what they know now. The insight of someone with experience as an administrator is invaluable for those aspiring to fill the same role. These observations are also useful in an interview to help make answers fuller and more relevant to the realities of the position.

# UPPER MANAGEMENT

# CHAPTER 13

# The Role of the Director

> Think of three Things—whence you came, where you are going,
> and to whom you must account.
>
> —BENJAMIN FRANKLIN (1732)

BENJAMIN FRANKLIN WAS A MAN WHO COULD SET GOALS, and achieve them. Among his many other strengths, the organized and collaborative way that he pursued the numerous hobbies, interests, and plans he made throughout his life led to a long list of achievements. One of his major contributions to American life is the founding of the first lending library in the United States, the Library Company of Philadelphia (Halford 2010). He even served as the company's librarian for a time. As he said about the success of this endeavor, "Our people, having no publick amusements to divert their attention from study, became better acquainted with books, and in a few years were observ'd by strangers to be better instructed and more intelligent than people of the same rank generally are in other countries" (Halford 2010). Franklin recognized the great potential of libraries to create an educated populace capable of participating in democracy. This vision, coupled with his unceasing dedication to achieving goals, set in motion the great tradition of libraries in this country. As a leader, he understood the importance of buy-in, as well as the need to persuade others in order to achieve his goals. In 1776, Franklin was sent to France as a diplomat for the revolutionary colonies, and succeeded in winning the support of French nobility for the American cause. In part, he did so by wearing plain clothes and a simple fur hat that appealed to romantic notions of America as a frontier nation fighting for liberty.

Though Franklin is often not remembered as a leader in the same way the great generals and early presidents are, he stands out as a role model for future head librarians. His organization, vision, and ability to do the necessary hard work required for success model the most important attributes of a chief librarian, often called an executive director or dean. This is because the ultimate job of a director is to identify a vision for the library and to ensure that this vision is carried through, sometimes even in the face of resistance to change. Doing this is intimidating and can feel daunting, but the most successful directors are those who understand that "well done is better than well said," another of Franklin's adages. Excellent library directors identify goals, make a plan, and lead the library to achieve those ends. Directors who overthink it or let themselves be led rather than taking control aren't doing the work. This doesn't mean that a chief librarian should be megalomaniacal in consolidating power, but success at this level does require the confidence to make one's vision known—unambiguously—and to pursue it, as well as the interpersonal skills to persuade others to see this vision and support it.

This can be complicated because, though it may seem like the person in this role would have total authority and autonomy over a library, the reality is often closer to the experience of a head or deputy director. Communicating and working with the layer of management over the library, whether at a university, or in city government or a school district, is a chief responsibility. The director must get buy-in from the executive leadership in regard to the proposed vision, because buy-in leads to the necessary resources to realize it. A lack of buy-in ensures that the library won't get what it needs. As a result, this position requires someone who can negotiate the relationship between the executive leadership of the larger organization, garnering more support, better resources, and true understanding. The successful director is able to articulate a vision, define the steps required to realize it, and convince others to support it in meaningful ways.

For this reason, and many others, the role of the head librarian is all about communication. This is reflected in "Academic Library Directors: What Do They Do?" by Peter Hernon, Ronald R. Powell, and Arthur P. Young (2004) The authors found that some of the most reported activities of library directors over a twelve-day period included fundraising, meeting other university administrators, handling personnel matters, meeting with library managers, financial management, correspondence via email, and meetings with faculty and library staff. Notice that most of these activities involve interpersonal communication and collaboration. Being a director requires more meetings and collaborative work than at any other time in a person's career. This means finding new ways to be flexible with resources, ideas, goals, and a vision for the organization, skills that begin to develop with project management and middle management positions.

Dan Butin defines this role well in "So You Want to Be a Dean" (2016): "a dean is often in the unfortunate liminal position of being no longer truly a professor but not completely an administrator, either . . . and thus prone to role conflict and ambiguity." To put it another way, the chief librarian is sandwiched between upper administration and the rest of the library, much in the same way the middle manager is sandwiched between the director and other library staff. Because of this, in some ways a head librarian is no longer truly a librarian. This role pulls this person out of the library, especially if he or she is a good administrator. For a while, new directors might try to stay "in the trenches," working the reference desk on a regular basis or cataloging when they have a minute, but the longer someone stays a head librarian, the more they will find that they have to let some of these duties go. Directors work their whole career to be the best librarian they can, and when they finally make it to the lead role, their duties won't always have much to do with the library. Though this feels odd, it is a natural transition and a milestone in the trajectory of a manager's career away from practicing librarian and into administration, a journey that begins in middle management. Directors are called to serve in many ways throughout the organization, often outside of the library. This doesn't mean they aren't serving the library, too. What it does mean is that the role is outward-facing. The job is to gain visibility and respect that can be parlayed into goodwill and resources. The paradox is, of course, that even though the director may be called on to do things with little relevance to the library, he or she is also the chief library expert on campus or for the city. This role requires someone who is competent enough when it comes to librarianship to speak with authority and make rational decisions about the library when called on, but who can also fill a larger purpose in the organization as needed.

This is not the only paradox of the director's job. There are many other aspects that might surprise new directors, and two are particularly unique. The first is that, while directors attend more meetings with more people than ever before, they may also be lonelier than they have ever been. The second is that, while collaboration is a key trait of people who fill the role of library director, they are occasionally required to make decisions all on their own.

## Corner Office for One

There's an old saying: it's lonely at the top. Like many such sayings, this one is true. One big change from middle manager to library executive is that directors lose some of the camaraderie they had when their peers were in the library. To some degree, this is true anytime someone begins managing people, as discussed in the previous section, but it is especially true for the library director because there is no one else with a roughly equivalent position related to libraries. The director will almost certainly stop getting lunch invites, or at least get far fewer, and won't be invited to that movie over the weekend. Maybe former colleagues will forget to send emails about the staff book club. Jessica Lavariega Monforti and Javier Kypuros put it well in "10 Suggestions for a New Academic Dean" (2019): "Being a dean can be an isolating experience (remember: friendly but not friends)."

These things hurt, but they are necessary. Bosses can have warm and authentic relationships with their direct reports, but they probably aren't going to have the same friendships that they were used to as middle managers or individual contributors. That's the natural course of things, and it's something to anticipate. Directors have to make decisions, occasionally unilateral decisions, that may impact other library staff negatively, such as having to carry out a reduction in force where staff members must be let go, or cutting budgets. That is the job. Directors need to define these relationships, and ensure that there are enough boundaries to allow a healthy, productive repartee between them and the rest of the library, while still allowing for tough choices when necessary. Good boundaries go a long way toward getting the relationship with staff right.

That said, directors can still have some very meaningful relationships with their colleagues in different departments. Their new peers are other directors and deans across the organization. This won't provide the same daily interaction as with other middle managers within a library, but directors might find colleagues with whom they can be quite chummy. A deputy director might also become more of a colleague than a subordinate on a day-to-day basis. This can help to form a strong and strategically important alliance, since the director and deputy work together and have many of the same goals. Finally, the importance of professional groups becomes more outsized, because these allow networking with other chief librarians. Joining listservs reserved for upper management can be especially useful, such as a listserv for library directors across an entire university system or region.

## Being Bossy

A library director is the ultimate authority over the library. This means that directors are in a role where, if it is their prerogative, they can boss people around as much as they would like, within the confines of civility and reason. Obviously, in practice, an overly authoritarian approach is not going to go over well with the people who work in the library. Most people realize this before they become a director, but a chief librarian can't simply go in and tell everyone what to do all the time. Servant leadership is incredibly important, especially in academia. This means recognizing that, in some sense, the director works for the rest of the library staff and not the other way around.

Another treacherous pitfall, and one that is probably more common in libraries, is the tendency to undermanage situations. Per Linda Hill and Kent Lineback in *Being the Boss*, "to confuse being liked with being trusted or respected is a classic trap for all managers" (2019, 51). There are times when every director has to make a decision that is not popular. Maybe the majority of people disagree: doesn't matter. Sometimes, a director has to be the boss, and make the call.

The key, as with any superpower, is to use it sparingly and in the right situations. As an example, consider a library where a group of long-standing employees, both librarians and paraprofessionals, wants to retain and keep updating a physical card catalog as a "backup" to the online public access catalog (OPAC). This activity is taking an outsized amount of time that could be better spent elsewhere. The staff members are change-adverse and are protesting the decision to get rid of it. The director in this situation would almost certainly need to get rid of the catalog—it's a resource black hole, probably gets no use, and there are many, better kinds of backup for an OPAC. In this situation the director would overrule staff. Buy-in would be great, but ultimately it won't change the decision, and the director would need to be honest with the employees about that.

All this is to say that sometimes, one has to be bossy to be the boss. That's not always nice, not really fair, and not even a little egalitarian. It probably isn't what was taught in a management class in library school, and in the beginning it can make a new director feel really bad. But—and this is important—in the real world, it happens, and with some frequency. To be honest, this is probably why the director doesn't get invited to that book club anymore. The role of library director is singular and sometimes decisive. On the bright side, the staff is probably kind enough to act like they just forgot. Please don't take them at their word and show up anyway.

As much as each director wants to make the library staff happy, sometimes being a leader comes first. The reality is that many people cry in the office of every director—this is inescapable. They will cry because of interpersonal conflicts with fellow employees, because they are frustrated with their position, because they aren't doing their job well, because they are overwhelmed with joy over a promotion or, hopefully not too often, because the director has said something unintentionally insensitive. Always keep tissues on the desk, and when it's a bad kind of cry, remember that the job is to get the library where it needs to go. Not everyone is going to be on board with that, but one way or another, they need to be brought on board, because the director's job is to make sure that the library meets its goals and realizes its vision. Hopefully, this can be done with graciousness and kindness whenever possible. At these moments, a capable director reviews lessons learned that can help manage this situation, keeps an eye on where the library needs to go, and remembers that the organization has people to whom it is answerable. Put another way by one of our great early librarians, "Think of three Things—whence you came, where you are going, and to whom you must account" (Franklin 1732).

# References

Butin, Dan. 2016. "So You Want to Be a Dean?" *Chronicle of Higher Education*, January 13. https://www.chronicle.com/article/so-you-want-to-be-a-dean-234900/.

Franklin, Benjamin. 1732. *Poor Richard's Almanack*. Reprint, Mount Vernon, NY: Peter Pauper Press, 1984.

Halford, Macy. 2010. "'Reading Became Fashionable': Ben Franklin and the Privatization of Libraries." *The New Yorker*, September 27. https://www.newyorker.com/books/page-turner/reading-became-fashionable-ben-franklin-and-the-privatization-of-libraries.

Hernon, Peter, Ronald R. Powell, and Arthur P. Young. 2004. "Academic Library Directors: What Do They Do?" *College & Research Libraries* 65: 538–63. EBSCO Education Source.

Hill, Linda A., and Kent Lineback. 2019. *Being the Boss, with a New Preface: The 3 Imperatives for Becoming a Great Leader*. Boston: Harvard Business Review Press.

Lavariega Monforti, Jessica L., and Javier A. Kypuros. 2019. "10 Suggestions for a New Academic Dean." *Chronicle of Higher Education*, August 25. https://www.chronicle.com/article/10-suggestions-for-a-new-academic-dean/.

# Managing Managers and Managing Up

I N 1999, TINA FEY BECAME THE HEAD WRITER of *Saturday Night Live*, and has had a long career ever since as an executive producer, in addition to her better-known roles on screen. Her book *Bossypants* delves into many topics, including Fey's time as a leader. About being a boss, Fey wrote that "in most cases, being a good boss means hiring talented people and getting out of their way" (2011, 5). This idea is central to both managing managers, and managing up when reporting to someone outside of the library. Both contexts require trusting the people enough who work for the organization to let them do their jobs. For managers of managers, this means providing the tools, mentorship, and support that enables a direct report to succeed as managers themselves, and resisting the desire to become too involved in the day-to-day details. For directors as employees of someone outside the library, this means earning the good faith of the boss so that person can get out of the way. In both cases, winning trust is the key to building positive, productive relationships between layers of management.

At first glance, managing the human resources of the library at the executive level might not seem that much different than doing so in middle management. Many of the same issues arise, and are dealt with in a similar fashion. What may be novel is the new task of managing managers, which presents fresh pitfalls. Also unique is the fact that the director reports to someone who is a library "outsider" for the first time in his or her career. Whether a city manager, provost, or school principal, there is a good chance that this boss has never worked in a library. As the chief library officer at an institution, this makes the job more difficult, because issues relevant to the library must be explained with authority to an outside audience. This means that the director must defend the library's position as the only librarian in the room. For this reason, managing up becomes much more important. The boss can be a director's first and best ally outside of the library.

## Definitions

360-degree performance review: A work evaluation that gathers feedback from subordinates and colleagues, in addition to an employee's own manager.

Managing by wandering around: Management by meandering around the workplace in an unplanned manner to check in on employees, projects, and equipment.

Managing up: Influencing and assisting one's manager by understanding that manager's goals and stressors, and working to help them navigate these pressures.

Turnover: the rate of employee separations.

## Managing Managers

As mentioned above, many of the skills gained in managing staff and faculty also apply to managing managers. Managers need clears goals, strong career mentoring, and good feedback, just as other employees do. There are some additional considerations when managing managers, however. These include modeling excellent management, coaching middle managers to become library executives, and building skip-level relationships with employees who report to these mid-level managers.

As Linda Hill and Kent Lineback note, the transition from manager to manager of managers is one of the most complicated transitions as a professional moves up the career ladder, but it is also one of least recognized (2019). This is because many people assume that it is more of the same responsibilities a director had in lower-level positions as a supervisor to practitioners. The more complicated nature of this task is evident, however, when considering a common scenario for a manager of managers: a direct report who is doing the functional duties of the job exceptionally well, but is having serious difficulties working with staff members.

In this case, managers at the middle level, who mostly deal with individual contributors, generally know if someone is doing the job or not, and that is the main concern. If someone doesn't get along well with others, but this is not the main focus of the position, then it may not cause serious problems or require intervention by the supervisor. On the other hand, managers who are not getting along well with their subordinates can cause a host of problems for a director, and this needs to be addressed quickly. Staff turnover in particular is a big issue, since poor management is a morale killer. The director needs to spend time working with this manager to improve his or her performance. In addition, the director likely needs to take on some of the softer supervisory duties related to these employees, especially mentorship if trust has been damaged. As this example shows, when the situation involves a manager, a simple problem with socialization is much more complicated.

This is all to say that the transition to manager of managers is hugely impactful, but not often recognized. By focusing on the three skills mentioned earlier—modeling, coaching, and team-building—new directors can further develop the skills they learned as mid-level managers and grow these skills to achieve success in upper administration.

## Modeling

In the aptly named *Superbosses*, Sydney Finklestein identifies modeling good behaviors as one important characteristic of great bosses (2016). Excellent managers of managers show their employees how to be supervisors by doing it themselves. Employees learn what to do as managers from their boss. They take their supervisor's management style as an example of what is expected. If their boss displays bad behaviors, employees pick those up. Likewise, if their boss treats them well, they see that and follow the example. Good librarians create good librarians; good managers create good managers.

This may seem obvious when put this way, but in practice it is not always clear. For instance, let's say a head of access services has discovered a pattern of similar mistakes occurring whenever a particular circulation assistant is on the desk. This assistant is charged with reserves and manages several student workers in this capacity. Though getting this pattern of mistakes corrected may seem like a relatively small matter, if the head of access services handles it wrong, this could model a pattern of behavior for the assistant that might then spill over into the way the student workers are treated. If the head is rude to the assistant, or corrects the assistant in front of patrons, then this shows the assistant that these behaviors are appropriate, even though they are discouraging and have a big impact on morale. If, instead, the head of access services sends a kind email or speaks to the assistant when they are off the desk or in another way that shows discretion, then the assistant learns something about how to treat the student workers.

Directors do this all the time, whether they recognize it or not. The way a director listens to other employees in staff meetings, for instance, models how direct reports are expected to listen when their respective staff have something to say. A director who is reluctant to give middle managers authority in the library teaches those middle managers that they aren't trusted, and creates a culture where the mid-level supervisors feel like they need to keep a close eye on what everyone else does, lest they lose even more of the director's confidence. Conversely, a director who shows great faith in subordinates gives those subordinates the confidence to, in turn, trust their own staff and give them more autonomy. New directors must take to heart that every action shows their direct reports how they expect them to be as leaders, in the same way that managers create organizational culture. Modeling the good behavior one expects is the fastest way to convey these expectations.

## Coaching

Finklestein also talks about the importance of apprenticeships. Per Finklestein, superbosses create strong, day-to-day relationships with their protégés (2016). These relationships differ from boss to boss, but they are authentic. As the chief library officer, a director must take a genuine interest in lower-level managers on a daily basis by asking them how they are getting along with their employees, helping them think through difficult situations, and getting to know them and how they manage. When managing managers, it is also important to ask them about all of the members on their team, problems they face, and inter-team conflicts. Being aware of these issues gives an idea of what is going on throughout the team. The way managers answer these questions also provides real insight into their anxieties, concerns, and feelings toward team members. Directors must really listen and think about these conversations, because they can reveal the right way to guide and mentor managers.

Consider a situation where a director has a background in electronic resources, but the e-resources librarian reports to the head of technical services rather than to the director. Though the e-resources librarian doesn't work directly for the director, this situation actually creates a great opportunity for the director to teach the head of technical services about the e-resources domain if that head doesn't have a lot of experience with it, and to mentor him or her in managing someone who works in e-resources. By checking in with this head regularly, the director can watch for problems and shape the outcomes in this area without having to openly intervene. This helps to ensure that the e-resources librarian receives the mentorship needed to develop professionally, while also making the technical services head a better mid-level manager by broadening professional competencies. This situation, which may seem difficult on the surface, can be an ideal opportunity for everyone involved to grow. A director who, instead, jumps into a direct mentorship relationship with the employee risks cutting out the manager, and they won't have the same day-to-day interaction they might otherwise have. Even worse, a director who simply leaves it up to the head of technical services to muddle through alone risks missing issues as they emerge, that may later grow into major problems, which are always more difficult to manage.

## Team-Building

As a manager of managers, team-building becomes more complicated and more important. Be visible and approachable, even for those who are not direct reports. Most people have probably heard of management by "wandering around." This is a good place to start, but it probably isn't enough. If possible, meet with people who work for direct reports on a semi-annual basis, without their manager, to check in and see how things are going. These meetings should focus tactfully on the relationship with their manager, as well as on what their career goals are and whether the library is helping to prepare them to reach these goals. This is useful for picking up on tensions with a supervisor, but it can also help the director see where there might be opportunities to grow an employee. Often directors have a higher-level understanding of the opportunities across the library than middle managers, and may be able to ease the way for staff members to get valuable experience. For instance, the director may be able to offer reference or teaching practice to a paraprofessional in technical services who is going to library school, and who might not have those same opportunities within their own unit.

Implementing 360-degree performance reviews, where the team can provide anonymous feedback about the manager, is also useful because it can identify problems with a manager early, allowing the director to guide and mentor before the situation becomes too drastic. A 360-degree review means asking colleagues and employees of the manager to provide feedback about manager performance for a set period of time, usually through an anonymous survey or another, similar measure. A 360-degree review is similar to the satisfaction surveys so common in libraries, asking someone's employees and peers to rank how well the manager is doing the job. As with other kinds of surveys, structured and open-ended questions are both important to ensure that the survey is targeting skills that are meaningful to the director, while also providing the opportunity for input outside of what the survey creator anticipated.

In addition to these formal actions, remember that sometimes just being around is the key. Always participate in potlucks, parties, and other staff activities when possible. This builds a sense of camaraderie and helps the director connect with people in an authentic and low-key setting where they don't feel put on the spot. Directors who cater a staff appreciation event once or twice a year may find that it's worth every penny to build trust and get to know skip-level employees better.

# ⊚ Managing Up

Managing up refers to the practice of working with one's direct supervisor with an aim to make the supervisor's goals more achievable and stressors easier to handle. Managing up, in this context, is ultimately about getting buy-in. Like Franklin in his homespun suit, good library directors identify the best way to appeal to those above them. Every librarian has heard stories at some point in their career about city managers, provosts, or principals who simply did not value the library—those who cut budgets routinely, or who didn't support a director's goals. Creating a relationship with the administrator directly above the library, as a director, is about avoiding this fate. Remember, if the provost or city manager has a good relationship with the director, this translates into a good opinion of the library overall. As Mary Abbajay says in *Managing Up*, this "is not about brown-nosing, sucking up, or becoming a sycophant," but about "consciously and deliberatively developing and maintaining effective relationships with supervisors, bosses, and other people above you in the chain of command" (2018, 1).

## Know Your Manager

There are lots of resources written about figuring out what type of boss one has and how best to work with that supervisor. What these resources equate to is, know the boss. Know the boss's likes or dislikes, pet peeves, goals, the pressures from managers, and issues the boss is trying to solve. Learn the administrator's communication style and preferences for frequency of meetings and updates.

In the context of the library, the biggest thing to know is how the boss views libraries, both the specific library and libraries in general. The view that administrators have of libraries shapes why they may or may not value them. If, for instance, the boss believes that libraries are a cornerstone of research across campus, then requests for resources can be shaped to answer how these funds further the research agenda of the institution. If the boss sees libraries as a civic good, educating those in the community to meaningfully participate in a democratic society, then resource requests could target the educational or civic roles of the library. If, in contrast, the administrator views the library as an out-of-date money pit that many people no longer use, the library director can focus on showing the administrator the way libraries help bridge the digital divide, or how high library usage is by the community, hopefully changing this view. In all of these cases, the key is understanding what the administrator values about the library, or could potentially value, and working to frame appeals based on this understanding.

## Help Your Manager

A director who knows the boss knows how to help the boss. Make a list of all of the strategic objectives the administrator has for the organization, and the problems the boss is facing in achieving these objectives, particularly those problems that might be causing pressure from above. Ask which of these objectives can the library help achieve and which problems can the library solve. Show, whenever possible, how the administrator's interests and the library's activities align. The administrator above the library is often the single most important person in the organization as far as determining the resources and support the library receives. It's important that he or she understands how those resources actually benefit the organization's overall vision, helping to achieve goals and solve problems. Most directors can think of a hundred ways the library does this, but it must be communicated clearly, because the person above the library likely hasn't ever been a librarian and doesn't have the same innate understanding of what libraries do.

As an example, many cities have a problem with teenagers hanging out after school and getting into trouble around town. This might be one area of concern for a city manager, who wants to create meaningful activities to occupy these kids in positive and productive ways. This problem might also spill over to the library, where some of these teenagers might come and make trouble after school. The library could create a work skills program for this group, teaching them valuable competencies while also giving them meaningful activities after school. This program solves a library problem, provides more manpower for the library to achieve its other goals, and also addresses concerns the administrator already has. If this program is communicated well to the city manager, it could be viewed as a real asset.

The other side of this is that directors need to avoid creating problems for their managers. Handle library problems in the library, whenever possible. Have an employee who is underperforming? Ask for input, but don't expect the administrator to handle the problem. Avoid letting problems get so big that these become the administrator's issue. Even when a problem requires approval from someone higher up to solve, make that as easy as possible. Suppose the library has a hole in the roof. Come up with multiple strategies to fix the problem, with multiple costs. Identify the strengths and weaknesses of each solution. Present them to the administrator, so that he or she has as little to do as possible, and then work with the chief financial officer to schedule the construction.

Helping one's boss also means agreeing to projects or assignments that may be extraneous to one's main job. If asked to run a search committee for the head of another department, for instance, say yes. This not only helps the boss, but also demonstrates that one can act as the organization's representative in this capacity. If asked to head a working group for space use in city buildings, again, say yes. When issues related to space come up, the head of this working group is always solicited for input, giving this person a voice in important decisions. In other words, rather than playing defense when the parks department tries to take over the vacant lot earmarked for a new branch library, the library director, acting as the space management committee head, can ensure the library's needs are considered. This is to say that, while a director might not immediately see the value, and might not be able to commit in every instance, saying yes some of the time is essential, especially for high-profile requests.

## Disagree and Commit

Amazon has a management concept called "have backbone—disagree and commit." This is a good concept for anyone when working with a supervisor, but especially for new directors. What this means is, there are times when an executive makes an unpopular decision, or a decision with which the director just doesn't agree. When one is a middle manager working in a unit, one can complain about that decision and disavow it. As a director, even if it really wasn't an agreeable decision, it has to be enforced—it becomes the management's decision. As if this wasn't uncomfortable enough, the director can't go around the library complaining about it and undermining the big boss. The decision must be carried out faithfully. It is always difficult when one is tasked with carrying out a disagreeable policy, and often, disagree and commit is required. Directors must make clear they disagree with the decision to the provost or city manager, but trust the decision-making and commit to seeing it through if the boss doesn't change his or her mind.

The first part of this imperative—have backbone, disagree—means letting the boss know there is disagreement. Though some administrators might like "yes men," hopefully this boss isn't one of them. It is vital that employees tell their boss when he or she is making a bad decision. A director with good judgment, who tells a provost or city manager when they are wrong, is worth his or her weight in gold, especially since people in these positions might not get this type of honesty often. Many less-than-brilliant ideas get shot down by dedicated direct reports with a better understanding of the issue than the executive. Absolutely have backbone, and disagree when needed.

Sometimes, though, when a director disagrees, the provost or city manager may still decide to follow through with the decision. If the concerns are voiced, discussed thoroughly, and the executive has decided to proceed as planned, trust that person enough to commit to that course of action. This means full dedication to making a decision work, not complaining about the decision to fellow employees or constantly pointing out that there was disagreement. Support the thinking of the executive management. Obviously, this will not work in a situation where the decision is illegal or unethical—in those situations, librarians have a professional duty not to commit, but rather to go to HR or even the police. Most situations, however, are a simple difference of opinion. Once the decision is made, commit to seeing it through, and take a gamble on an executive's intuitions. This shows the boss that the director has enough confidence in the administrator to go along with the plan, which in turn fosters confidence in the director.

## Management Team

As commit and disagree suggests, directors are, in some sense, no longer simply members of the library staff. Their words have authority, and people take them seriously. Directors need to comport themselves in a way that befits this status. This is to say that, while some might have complained about a boss, or a new policy, or a coworker as a lower-level librarian, as a director or even a manager, the best course is to think deeply about what is expressed to the rest of the library. People pay attention. Directors are responsible for setting the morale of the library.

As a member of the university or city management team, sometimes big or controversial decisions need to be made. Reaching consensus among the leaders of major departments can be an effective way to make sure that issues are considered appropriately. Again, if decisions are made this way, any disagreements should be kept within the management group. The administration of the larger organization is a team, and once the decision is made, the team needs to implement it and support it. In order to manage, all members need to know that they can be frank and honest in discussions. Members who violate the built-in trust due to lack of discretion are not fulfilling their roles.

That said, when decisions are made this way, there must be meaningful opportunities for input so people don't feel like they are cut off from management. Sometimes the impulse to share disagreements from these kinds of meetings is based on the desire to draw back the curtain so that other members of the staff understand the management's thinking. There are other, better ways to ensure input, which ideally should happen before the decision is made. Remember that undermining the management of the organization creates big morale issues that are difficult to fix once entrenched, and that issues of morale will fall to the provost or city manager. Just like committing to the decisions a big boss makes shows confidence in the organization's leadership, so does committing to decisions made by the management group.

## Prepare

Prepare means two things: prepare for meetings and other communications with the boss, and prepare the boss for potential problems down the road. Preparing for meetings and other communications is pretty self-explanatory, but it's worth exploring. Set an agenda for meetings with the supervisor. Though there may be some discussions focused on areas of concern to the boss, on the whole these meetings should give the director a chance to explore questions and concerns. Make a list before each meeting and guide the conversation. This ensures that the director has a clear indication of the boss's feelings, and shows that the director respects the administrator's time enough to use it wisely.

The second meaning of prepare is prepare the boss whenever a potential problem becomes evident. As Michael Singer Dobson and Deborah Singer Dobson note in *Managing Up!*, don't ever let your boss be blindsided (Dobson and Dobson 2000). When you bring up a potential problem, also identify the solution. For instance, some academic libraries have issues with bed bugs. The minute a book with bed bugs is identified, email the administrator over the library and let him or her know, so they aren't shocked by fumigation costs or bed bug ovens later on. Let's say the library has to be evacuated because of a suspicious, unattended item. Sometimes, in these scenarios, campus police call the local fire department. Email or text the administrator right away, as he or she may see or hear the firetrucks speeding toward the library. What if a student is arrested for something in the library? Let the boss know. Maybe baby rattlesnakes were found in the stacks. There is likely a nest somewhere in the building, and they hatched. Let the provost know! Even sensitive issues with library staff that might become more complicated down the road could be important for a boss to know about. Never let the boss find out about a situation like one of these after it becomes a huge problem. Prepare the boss for the worst, but hope for the best, and have plenty of recommendations when things go wrong.

## Accept Responsibility

As chief library executives, directors need to get in the habit of accepting responsibility. This means a few different things. For one, it means accepting responsibility when things go wrong. Don't blame staff, or the boss, or another department. Every problem in the library is ultimately the director's responsibility, and the director must search out and coordinate a response. This is difficult! Library directors have to rely on the managers below them, and the people who work for them. If anyone at any layer makes a big mistake, ultimately—whether it was the director's fault or not—he or she is responsible. Sometimes that feels really unfair, but move past that and accept it with grace.

This also means that, except on rare occasions where a fix cannot happen without higher-level intervention, the director is responsible for ensuring that the library works. The library's problems should not be the administrator's problems. President Truman purportedly kept a sign on his desk that said "The buck stops here." That should be the director's motto for the library. Ideally, after a few months, the boss—whether provost, city manager, or principal—should be able to tell people that the library runs itself because it takes so little of his or her time. Middle managers have the ability to let the director take responsibility. Directors no longer have this luxury. They are responsible for the library, full stop. If the director is doing the job right, then the boss should trust the director enough to get out of the way.

## Expressing Needs

Even after trying all these approaches for managing up, no one can control what type of supervisor one has, and for a director, the provost or city manager often determines how enjoyable, or even tolerable, the job is. Even those who shop around and accept a job with a great upper administration might find, years down the line, that the university has hired someone new with whom they don't get along. While this chapter could endeavor to provide a typology of leaders and give advice about how to work with each type, the reality is that people don't fit into neat little boxes. Someone, somewhere has stumbled across that rare city manager who is both authoritarian and laissez-faire, or charismatic and bureaucratic. People aren't typologies, and what it comes down to in every case is if the employee isn't working well with a supervisor or getting what is needed from the work relationship, then the employee must be proactive and express this to the boss. Knowing leadership styles, covered in chapter 2, can certainly help approach this issue, but employees who sublimate their own needs for their supervisor's preferences are not happy or satisfied. The most direct solution is to make sure that the boss knows what kind of supervisor is required. The employee is his or her own best advocate. When issues occur, take control of the situation as much as possible, and clearly state what is amiss in a respectful way, while asserting an openness to working together to make the situation exceptional rather than suboptimal.

This is easier to understand in a real-life situation. Consider a provost asking a new director to hire an administrative assistant, without specifying what the position is for, how many hours, or the salary. The director may have never posted a position before, and doesn't know how to do it. This director would need to make a list of questions about the position, seek clarification in the form of a meeting or email, and seek out someone in HR to explain how to post it. If the director felt like the supervisor was not providing enough support in executing the request, the pair could have a conversation explaining how the director learns best and asking how the provost wants to receive questions or concerns in the future. This director would be turning a seemingly nebulous task into an important learning experience, and the provost will get to know the new director's style.

Conversely, the provost may provide too much oversight and instruction, more than the new employee wants. Perhaps the director is a kinesthetic learner who needs to try to do things to learn them, and therefore, requires more freedom in reaching a stated end goal. Though the situation is different, the solution is the same: clearly communicate that the needs of the new manager aren't being met.

Even with this direct approach, a supervisor may continue to ignore the employee's needs. Old habits are hard to break and, unfortunately, some managers just aren't motivated to work with staff. Perhaps the city manager was asked to provide better communication, but continues to make decisions verbally and then contradict herself when a question is asked later. Even in this case, the director can be proactive and write a follow-up email after the meeting to confirm what was said. Again, if the problem gets bad enough, there's always another job.

The point is that directors have control over their work and their relationship with the boss. Sometimes, new library directors see the upper administrator as intimidating because they may not have reported to someone ranked this highly in previous jobs. The provost or city manager, in this case, is also a direct supervisor. Directors must approach them as such, making sure their needs are clearly expressed and met.

## Key Points

- Management at the level of director is about trust—gaining trust in one's middle managers, and getting trust from higher-level administrators.
- Though the transition to managing managers isn't often recognized, it is an important step in the professional growth of a library leader.
- Managers of managers should use modeling, coaching, and team-building to navigate the complicated relationships with their direct reports, as well as their skip-level employees.
- Managing up can be a good way for a library director to gain the trust of the administrator over the library.

## References

Abbajay, Mary. 2018. *Managing Up: How to Move Up, Win at Work, and Succeed with Any Type of Boss*. Hoboken, NJ: Wiley. EBSCO eBook Collection.

Dobson, Michael Singer and Deborah Singer Dobson. 2000. *Managing Up!: 59 Ways to Build a Career-Advancing Relationship with Your Boss*. New York: AMACOM. EBSCO eBook Collection.

Fey, Tina. 2011. *Bossypants*. New York: Little, Brown and Company.

Finklestein, Sydney. 2016. *Superbosses: How Exceptional Leaders Master the Flow of Talent*. New York: Portfolio/Penguin.

Hill, Linda A. and Kent Lineback. 2019. *Being the Boss, with a New Preface: The 3 Imperatives for Becoming a Great Leader*. Boston: Harvard Business Review Press.

# Crisis Leadership

L IBRARIES BUILT IN THE PATH OF HURRICANES sometimes look a little different. Take the Mary and Jeff Bell Library at Texas A&M University–Corpus Christi. Constructed with a minimal number of windows, particularly on the first floor, the library is designed to weather a storm. This design is advantageous given the campus's close proximity to the Gulf of Mexico. When major hurricanes roll in, such as Hurricane Harvey in August 2017, the staff and faculty know how to jump into crisis preparations. Using plastic sheeting to cover the stacks and evacuating priceless archival materials to higher ground (Cummings 2020), the library ensures that whatever its fate might be, it is well prepared to endure.

Though most libraries are not so directly in the path of danger as TAMU–CC, at some point in their career, all library administrators face a crisis. This could be a budget cut, natural disaster, or facility failure, but all of them feel, in the moment, like an unsurmountable challenge. Despite the momentary sense of doom the director feels as the outline of the crisis becomes clear, libraries do eventually recover and move on with business as usual. The key is keeping a cool head and a steady hand. Remember, many people can manage at the best of times, and seem perfectly capable doing it. Leaders who can function in a crisis, and help their library survive, are a special bunch.

# Definitions

Crisis communication: Communications that occur during a crisis, and especially a crisis that involves reputational damage to the organization.

Crisis or disaster plan: A plan libraries create to define how they respond to different types of crises.

Disaster scenarios: Potential crisis situations that might befall an organization.

Drill: An exercise where a library practices the protocols in a disaster plan.

FEMA: The Federal Emergency Management Agency handles disaster response in the United States.

Tabletop exercise: An exercise where a library acts out a response to a disaster scenario, based on the disaster plan, to test how likely the plan is to work.

# Libraries in a Crisis

The fact that libraries need to function in a crisis might not be immediately clear. Some people don't realize how pivotal libraries are for their communities in times of crisis. Many cities and other municipalities in hurricane zones, for instance, require libraries to reopen soon after disasters, whenever possible, to act as community hubs of information and resource distribution, as well as places to charge electronics and jump on the internet in the immediate aftermath. Academic libraries are also key in the disaster plans for their campuses. During the coronavirus pandemic, as an example, many university libraries were pivotal to ensuring that students could continue to access the requisite digital resources to support research and coursework, often with little preparation. Some libraries are even built as storm shelters for their local communities. This is all to say that, though it may not be immediately clear that libraries are directly involved in disaster response, they are often central to it.

For this reason, anyone in a leadership position at a library must be mentally prepared to handle a potential crisis. Directors must think through what their response might look like. This might extend to the support a library could provide to the entire region. For instance, many libraries across Central Texas were asked to act as FEMA meeting locations after Hurricane Harvey hit the Gulf Coast, since the area was a main evacuation point for those whose homes were flooded. This disaster didn't hit in the immediate vicinity of these libraries, but it did impact the entire region. Similarly, many university systems have crisis plans that propose strategies for the continuation of services and the evacuation of students from campus. These plans require libraries to think through how to continue offering services if the main library is inaccessible. This may include allowing students of the impacted campus to use a library facility at a sister campus in the same university system. Again, a library might be called on to assist with a disaster that isn't even local to that library.

Though most people who work in libraries would agree that they are essential to the communities they serve, it is also fair to say that librarians don't tend to consider themselves first responders. This is especially problematic because crisis situations, such as natural disasters, impact librarians in their personal lives, not just at work. Requiring staff to come into the library directly after their own homes and families were impacted is a difficult call. Some libraries in hurricane zones, especially those with very rare archives, might even require staff to remain at the facility during the storm, if it is not too serious. Managing the expectations of staff, and providing for flexibility of staffing so that those who are worst impacted can focus on their home situation, is extremely important. This is why having a disaster plan is pivotal. When plans are articulated, and staff know what to expect, disasters are much easier to handle.

# ⑥ Crisis Planning

A crisis plan outlines the steps a library will take to handle a given disaster. As discussed in the first chapter, these plans are important because they force library staff to think through all of the contingencies that might occur, and to prepare mentally to manage a crisis situation. The first step in an excellent crisis plan is to do research. Find out what crises have historically impacted the surrounding area, and what the larger response plans are in the community and at the university. Talk to emergency and risk management personnel who are directly involved in this planning on a larger scale to get an idea about the expectations for local libraries. Also, find out if the local area is an evacuation destination from other regions. Again, disasters don't just tax the resources of those who live in the immediate area of the disaster. Institutions in the vicinity that receive evacuees also need to be involved in the response.

The city or institution likely has multiple disaster plans, ranging from small local disasters such as tornados, active shooters, or chemical spills, to large regional or national disasters, such as severe hurricanes, earthquakes, wildfires, and pandemics. Moreover, if the institution is a major university, it likely has disaster plans covering a more exotic list of potential crises, including viral outbreaks from labs, nuclear material protocols, and other types of potential risks to health and safety that may not be common outside of institutions performing research.

Remember, disasters are not just pandemics, hurricanes, or wildfires, though those and other similar crises impact all libraries at one point or another. They also include financial cuts so significant they can jeopardize the stability of the library, or small everyday nuisances, like a pipe bursting in the ceiling of an old building over several rows of stacks, a microwave fire in the break room, or a roof leak. Never underestimate the damage any amount of smoke or water can do when it gets into a library. These are common scenarios for libraries, but they can certainly also be considered a crisis that must be handled immediately. One only need think of the appearance of bed bugs in a library to realize that something so seemingly small can cause major headaches for a director. Like the potential for a wildfire or a flood, these everyday nuisances only become worse if no one knows what to do when they occur.

The type of disasters that commonly occur in the region where a library is located directly impact the type of disaster plans required. The library may not need every potential disaster response planned if the institution or city has really solid plans for most major disasters. That said, the library does need its own plan for some potential problems that other areas of the city or institution might not cover. Case in point: every library should have a plan for the potential burst pipe mentioned above, as well as the problem of bed bugs. Both are very common, and need staff trained to handle them as soon as they are identified. Incidentally, the example of a burst pipe is an excellent reason to make sure someone is in the library almost every day, because the only thing worse than a pipe burst is a pipe burst that has been ongoing for many hours.

Once the most likely crises in the region are identified, as well as other potentially damaging scenarios, the next step is to create plans for these scenarios. Engage local risk management and disaster planning experts in the organization, as well as information from disaster planning resources, such as those documented by the American Library Association (ALA) (2020) and the Federal Emergency Management Agency (FEMA) (n.d.). Some governments and universities have resources available to help, and might even do drills or tabletop exercises for different scenarios in which the library could participate. Traditionally, good disaster recovery plans include the aforementioned scenarios, flexible response modules for these scenarios that act as contingency plans depending on how the disaster develops, a chain of command, a command post, clear communication channels, backup resources, ways to practice each scenario, and a protocol for post-crisis review. Library plans may not need all of these elements, but they should have, at a minimum, crisis response modules, a chain of command, and some indication of how modules fit with different crisis scenarios.

The best way to go about creating such plans is to pull together a group of people in the library who are directly impacted by any potential disaster. This likely includes people working throughout the library, including public services, technical services, and archives. Though some plans are difficult to create in a group, this is one that requires lots of different knowledge about many areas of operation, and as a result a group effort is required for the best results, especially for important potential disasters that are common in the region. Inviting individuals from other areas of an organization who work with disaster planning to take part is, again, also important. The process to create these plans should be structured. Having an easy-to-follow template for modules and other constituent parts is key, so these can be easily referred to in times of stress. The committee might also create a small reference booklet with disaster preparedness information for staff based on the information in the plan. This provides an easier entry point for those working on the front lines who need to learn the basics, but may not need every detail.

Crisis response modules are written descriptions of different types of reactions that might be required. These could include a module for locking down the library, a module for responding to water damage to materials, a module for contacting the police, and so forth. Practically speaking, each module should contain a detailed explanation of what the steps are in response to the crisis, what equipment (if any) is required to deploy the response, when the response would be applied, and who has the authority to institute it. These crisis modules can be simple or complex. A good example of such a module is a lockdown procedure. These days, most libraries probably have a lockdown procedure that is widely understood by the staff. These procedures almost always include a detailed, step-by-step guide to how patrons lock down, how patron-facing staff engage with patrons to achieve the lockdown, the tasks staff perform, who initiates it, and why. Responses to water incoming in the stacks or the need to evacuate campus should follow this same pattern.

Assigning authority is important in these documents. People are sometimes hesitant to act in crisis situations if they are uncertain of the authority they have to do so. By assigning authority in a way that is clear and direct, staff won't have to spend time overthinking their role. Make sure that authority is being assigned at the right level of decision-making. For instance, student workers probably shouldn't be allowed to make decisions about how to handle a book returned with a potential bomb in it, or even one that might contain bed bugs. A somewhat higher level of decision-making authority would be required, perhaps a supervisor or full-time employee. Staff should be well trained for emergencies. This might include offering training related to CPR or the use of defibrillators, how to handle a patron overdose, or what to do in an active shooter situation.

Another important element of these modules is the list of equipment required to implement them. Libraries, like houses, should have emergency kits. Though in most cases these kits are used to provide patrons with band-aids when they get really serious paper cuts, having a kit on hand is nonetheless important. A library emergency kit has three parts: a first-aid kit for people, a first-aid kit for materials, and an emergency management kit. The first-aid for people should be a bit more extensive than just a simple pack with band-aids, ibuprofen, and Neosporin. Well-prepared libraries have AED defibrillators, Stop the Bleed kits, and other specialized medical resources that could help save lives. Again, staff must be trained to use these if they are available in the library. The first-aid kit for materials should include any of the resources that are mentioned in the crisis modules related to material damage. For instance, if felt, fans, and weights are required to dry out books, they need to be on hand. Every library should make sure plastic sheeting is available at all times. No one wants to waste an hour running to Home Depot while water is coming into the stacks. The emergency management kit should also have resources needed if there is an active crisis in the library, like a fire. This might include flashlights or evacuation maps. It might also include the purchase of specialized equipment, like an evac-chair for wheelchair-bound patrons.

Sometimes, the library director might not be the primary staff member responsible for crisis planning. Many libraries have someone on staff who finds this topic to be really interesting. It is worth nurturing this interest, especially if crisis planning is not a particular interest of the director. FEMA and the American Red Cross both offer excellent training related to disaster preparedness and response that might make this person the local authority on the topic. As with anything else, letting someone who is well trained and likes the work take the lead on disaster planning and crisis preparations can help ensure that these are done right.

# Navigating Crises

No matter how good the plan is leading up to a crisis, when one hits, most administrators feel ill-prepared to face it. Though the threat of a massive budget cut, wildfire, direct hit from a hurricane, earthquake, pandemic, or other disaster is a constant theoretical for every library, most escape unscathed the majority of the time—until they don't. Remember, disasters are difficult. The response may not be clear. Directors lay awake at night wondering when to close the library as they see caseloads for a new virus rising in their area, or a wildfire creeping ever closer to the facility. Directors in hurricane evacuation zones watch storms form off the coast, and as the one that is heading right for them turns toward shore, wonder if they did everything they could to protect their libraries. There are always "what ifs" in every crisis. Communicating, taking one decision at a time, and taking care are the keys to surviving these situations intact.

## Crisis Communication

First off, strictly speaking, most library administrators probably won't be responsible for their own crisis communications with the public. Many institutions have a communications department that handles true crisis communications. Crisis communications are usually defined as communication in defense of an organization or employee when they have a reputational problem—in other words, the type of communication required when a scandal, public relations kerfuffle, or other issue arises that lowers the reputation of a library. Hopefully, at least for libraries that function as a part of a larger organization—and almost all do—crisis communications in this sense is handled by professionals who understand what to do. Library administrators should be very happy to have the advisement of these well-trained professionals, and should defer to their expertise whenever possible.

That said, much of the advice given for the type of crisis communications described above is also valuable for communicating during the kinds of crises discussed in this chapter. When a disaster hits a library, an administrator has to be able to maintain the trust of the staff while providing clear and accurate information. If the leader of a library seems unsure of the situation, the staff also feel unsure, and this can cause one crisis to spiral into others, such as when a budget cut leads to massive staff turnover, even if widespread layoffs aren't imminent. A director who conveys a sense of uncertainty may also undermine confidence in his or her leadership, making it harder to make substantial changes to operations, if needed. In a pandemic, for instance, employees who are required to continue working with the public have to trust the precautions that leadership is taking to ensure their safety, or the result could be a public services staff refusing to work with the public. Leaders must be able to convey that they are calm and in control, even in stressful times.

This does not mean hiding worry and concern from staff. As with so many other elements of leadership, honesty is key to building trust in difficult times. In a financial crisis, when staff know that the library is going to get a budget cut, lying about it and saying everything is fine doesn't give staff much reassurance. A leader who communicates that, though budget cuts are coming, the library is taking concrete steps to prepare for the potential worst-case scenarios is much more trustworthy, because such a message acknowledges the reality. This does not mean that a leader in a time of crisis should scare people or let his or her own anxiety impact the way the crisis is discussed. Rather, cautious optimism coupled with concrete actions and transparency about how those actions help, and what the leader expects, goes a long way to build trust while keeping staff morale from sinking. This is one reason why it is important to cultivate the confidence of employees before a crisis ever hits—it is much harder to create trust in the middle of anxiety and stress.

Hand in hand with trust is the need to respond quickly, but carefully. Responding quickly is key because controlling the narrative is important. If staff are left without direction, uncertain of what is going to happen or what has already happened, they try to find their own solutions, and these might not be optimal. For instance, if a wildfire is near campus, and staff have no idea of whether or when they are supposed to close the library, they might leave it too long and put themselves and patrons at risk of injury, or close far too soon and risk ire from the city's upper management. In a financial crisis, if staff are left to guess at what might happen, rumors start to run rampant about potential budget cuts, significantly impacting staff morale. A leader needs to step into the informational void before other people try to fill it with speculation, hearsay, or conjecture.

That said, responding quickly does not mean responding recklessly. Giving poor or inaccurate information to staff, again, undermines trust. Directors must know how to give the information they have, and should know when to give updates simply to say there are no updates, but more information will come soon. Though this may seem like meaningless work, it reassures staff that things are happening in the background to manage the situation. For example, the director of a public library in an area recently hit by a hurricane might send out a quick message the morning after to remind staff of what they need to do and where they need to be, and to give a brief summary of the state of the library as far as he or she understands it. Obviously, in that moment, the director likely won't have much information about potential damage, but hearing from the director and having a reminder of the next few actions to take is an important touchstone.

In this case, the worst thing a director could do is convey inaccurate information, reassuring the staff, for instance, that there was relatively little damage when the roof was actually ripped off the building. Reading communications two, three, or four times to make sure everything is absolutely and certainly true is essential. Again, the trust of the staff is the biggest asset a director has.

Beyond cultivating trust and responding quickly, the tone of communications from directors in these moments should be both resolute and compassionate. Showing one's own humanity in a time of crisis, and making sure staff know that their personal trials mean something to the larger organization, goes a long way. In some cases, such as in a pandemic, this is absolutely essential to reassure staff. If staff members don't believe that administrators have their best interests at heart and will protect them as much as possible, it is difficult to continue to provide services.

## Make One Decision, Then Another

Though outwardly an administrator should present as resolute and confident in a crisis, internally, the landscape is likely far less certain. Navigating a crisis as a director is like rowing down difficult rapids in a little rubber boat; one feels ill-prepared, and the challenges just keep coming. There is no time to think about long-term planning or goals as there is only room for immediate concerns. Moreover, no matter how good a crisis plan is, there are always a million things that were not considered. It's the difference between thinking about how a library might fight a pandemic in theory, and guessing at how such a virus might be spread, versus the reality of a virus having a pathology that might not match one's guesswork during the planning phase. Another way to think about this is planning what happens if a hurricane hits the library, without factoring in the unlikely possibility that the levees might fail. In the specific scenario where the hurricane hits, and the levees do fail, all of the planning might be for naught. Librarians, as a profession of like-minded people, are well known for being planners. Crises can't really be planned.

This is all to say that a director can only make one decision at a time, and in a crisis, the sightline might only be the next decision. That's OK. Sometimes, getting through the situation at hand is, truly, the only thing that matters. This will likely cause a good deal of anxiety for library administrators with robust long-term plans. The key is managing the anxiety, because there isn't an alternative. Administrators who try to think too many steps ahead will get overwhelmed by the unknowns.

## Take Care

Take care of employees. Take care of patrons. Take care. In a budget cut, save jobs where possible, first and foremost. In a hurricane, find out if staff are OK and send care packages to those who lost their homes. In a pandemic, make patrons wear masks to take care of themselves and staff. Do the right thing, whatever it is, in the situation that presents itself. This may seem obvious, and it might be, but if the director doesn't take care of the people who make the library function, the library won't make it through.

Another way of thinking about this is, what are the stressors and problems staff and patrons are facing because of this? During the coronavirus pandemic, for instance, working from home with children, family members at risk, and the stress of constant remote communication was a frequent stressor. During Hurricane Harvey in Houston, it was the utter devastation to so many homes and library facilities. During a budget crisis, it is the loss of resources to support services, and the potential loss of jobs. Remember that crises frequently happen together. What can the library do to alleviate some of these stressors? Sometimes, this is as simple as giving someone a break by letting them take a day or two off. Sometimes, it might mean more substantial assistance through employee programs, local crisis assistance, or other resources. Whatever is needed, the library should not be one more weight at the worst time in an employee's or a patron's life. In addition to staff and patrons, directors should make sure that they are in the right place, mentally and emotionally, to lead. This means self-care.

## ◎ After the Storm

When a crisis is over, there should be a post-crisis review that looks at how the crisis plan was implemented—what worked and what didn't. This might not need to be super formal, but it does need to occur. If the planning done before the crisis did not meet the occasion, the crisis planning process should be reviewed, and altered to try to account for this issue. This review should also look at what really worked, and those elements should be incorporated into other crisis planning documents. For instance, if the chain of command made communication much easier, that same chain of command could be included in other plans. This step can be quite brief, but it is important if the library is to learn from the experience and move forward.

Also remember that crises have a tendency to bring people together, or pull them apart. Sometimes, it seems like they are doing both things at once! This review doesn't need to only focus on the logistics of the crisis, but also on what was learned about the staff, and the conditions under which they do their best work. What did everyone find out about themselves through this process? What was gained in terms of staff cohesion and morale, and what was lost? Sometimes, these questions are just as important as the operational ones because of the significant mental and emotional toll that crises can take.

While this review doesn't need to be formal, it likely needs to be written down. By writing down the facts of the experience, and what was learned from it, the library creates a document that can transfer this knowledge to successive leaders who may face similar disasters. Many calamities such as hurricanes and earthquakes generally only happen at long intervals. The same leader isn't likely to face an identical threat. This knowledge transfer is, then, particularly important, as the experience is a significant part of the institution's history.

This is true not just for the institution, but for the profession. Writing down experiences dealing with major crises, and publishing them in professional literature, is an important part of sharing knowledge with others in the field. Though one director might not face a direct strike from a hurricane twice, it is likely that at least one library director every year will experience this. When a director who has already gone through it passes on what was learned, the next director in line will have a better idea of what to expect, and how to handle it.

Libraries are also in the unique position to help their communities recover from crises, even after the danger has passed. TAMU–CC, for instance, started gathering archival materials about Hurricane Harvey even before the storm landed, an effort that has developed into the institution's Hurricane Harvey Oral History Collection (Cummings 2020). Remembering the disasters that impact libraries, as well as the ways these disasters were overcome, is also an act of memorializing the crises that define the communities a library serves. The ability to act as the memory of the larger region is one of the sacrosanct roles that a library plays, and this role is never more important than during a tragedy.

## Key Points

- All directors face some kind of crisis during their careers.
- Libraries are often essential services in the aftermath of a crisis, and directors should be mentally prepared to serve in this capacity.
- Crisis planning is the process that libraries use to prepare for a disaster.
- Crisis plans are made of a wide variety of flexible modules that define different types of disaster responses.
- Every library should have an emergency preparedness kit.
- Trustworthy and honest communication with staff is important during a crisis.
- Taking care of staff during a crisis keeps morale up.
- Post-crisis reviews are essential to ensure that the knowledge gained from a crisis is passed on to others at the institution and in the profession.

## References

American Library Association. 2020. "Disaster Preparedness and Recovery." http://www.ala.org/advocacy/disaster-preparedness.

Cummings, Marissa. 2020. "A Look Back at Hurricane Harvey's Impact in the Coastal Bend." *KIIITV*, August 25. https://www.kiiitv.com/article/news/a-look-back-at-hurricane-harveys-impact-in-the-coastal-bend/503-79556696-0870-4747-b6cb-29861d99bbcb.

Federal Emergency Management Agency. n.d. "FEMA Media Library." Accessed November 20, 2020. https://www.fema.gov/multimedia-library.

# Budgeting

OR MOST NEW DIRECTORS, AND ESPECIALLY THOSE who have never been involved in a formal budgeting process, handling the library's money can seem like a monumental challenge. Though everyone manages a household budget, those budgets are rarely hundreds of thousands or multiple millions of dollars, and are not subject to the institutional or governmental rules that libraries follow. This is exacerbated by the fact that financial management education in the library and information science curricula is often "disturbingly weak," as the findings of Robert Burger, Paula Kaufman, and Amy Atkinson attest (2015).

Budgeting is also fraught because it requires leaders to make difficult decisions that may turn employees against them. Stories abound of the new boss who comes in and starts cutting funding right away. Often, librarians have no sympathy for these bosses, who were likely faced with immediate, unanticipated, and difficult decisions. The good news is that, as a director, budgeting should become a natural part of the annual pattern of the year, the same as spring break, summer reading, or the first week of school. The bad news is that it requires a little math.

These general best practices should help directors plan for and manage monetary resources. They are commonsense suggestions learned on the job, rather than a deeply technical discussion of budgeting approaches and techniques. There are some excellent resources that do discuss the technical side of the budgeting process for libraries, and recommendations for those resources abound for those who want to pursue further reading.

## Definitions

Benchmarking: Using data from peer (or similar) institutions to determine appropriate expenditures for different expense categories.

Formula budgeting: A budget approach where statistical inputs determine formulaic budget allocations.

Incremental budgeting: A budgeting approach that starts with the previous budget, where only changes to the previous budget period's expenditures are reviewed.

Line-item budget: A budget that sets out allocations for each budget category, line by line, against the overall amount in each account.

Performance budgeting: A budget approach whereby performance outputs lead to budget allocations or budget cuts.

Program budgeting: A budget approach whereby strategic goals and vision determine budget allocations.

Separation of duties: The concept in auditing stipulating that duties related to money must be spread across multiple employees to ensure oversight, and that funds are not misappropriated.

Zero-based budgeting: A budgeting approach that starts at zero for each budget category, where all allocations must be requested and defended, even if they were in the previous budget.

## ⑥ Creating a Budget

Practically speaking, the first step to creating a new budget is deciding on a format. Chances are the institution uses financial software that shows a series of confusing credits and debits, how much the library has, and in which accounts, probably not in real time. This may seem like Greek to the majority of administrators, and is not meant to be a true line-item budget. Instead, this is what the larger organization uses to track the institution's finances at the macro level. A line-item budget is required—something simple enough to show how much is in each account, how much to spend on various categories, and how much to keep in reserve for when things inevitably go pear-shaped. It doesn't have to be more complicated than that. In *Library Management 101*, Lisa K. Hussey and Diane Velasquez provide a particularly simple discussion of how to create a line-item budget (2019).

Finding a way to set up a line-item budget so that it makes sense is extremely important. This doesn't necessarily require expensive budgeting software. For those who are familiar with Microsoft Excel or Google Docs spreadsheets, either might suffice. Just create a spreadsheet that tracks total allocations for each account, and then deduct the amount for each category of expenditure from the total allocation. The remainder in the account is represented at the bottom.

A line-item budget doesn't have to be anything more than this. Some people may not work well with spreadsheets. Budgeting software, or a table created in Microsoft Word, might be easier for those people. The key is to find the method of budgeting that makes the best sense to the director—one that can be tracked and followed. If the director doesn't understand the budget, or can't manipulate it without someone else's help, there will be problems.

The second important thing is to find the person working for the organization who understands budgets really well. Every institution has rules about budgeting that define what can be done and how much autonomy administrators have to do it. For instance, funding that comes from a state government is usually highly restricted in terms of how it is used, especially for things like travel or organizational memberships. Operational funds may be earmarked for fixed budget categories, such as heating or electricity. Money needs to be set aside for each employee line related to benefits. The amount to be set aside depends on the organization and the employee. There is someone working for the organization who knows all of this already, and the director's job is to buy that person a coffee and see what guidance he or she can provide. When it comes to budgeting, institutional knowledge is worth its weight in gold.

One thing to find out from this person is information about the organization's budget cycle. The institution likely has an annual budget request process that details how new money is requested every year, and when it can be expected. In addition to information about the budget cycle, there are other important things to know, such as:

- When does the money drop into the account every year? What happens if there are potential expenses before the money drops into the account?
- What happens if the library goes over budget?
- When does the library need to finish spending money? Will it lose money if it doesn't spend it?
- Will the budget be reduced if the library doesn't spend everything during the previous fiscal year?
- What happens if the library spends the full allocation, but doesn't get the amount allocated because student fees or taxes are lower than anticipated?

Some accounts may have different rules compared to others. Purchasing may require that the library stop spending funds for some period of time at the end of each fiscal year. Knowing this information is key for budget planning and review.

Finally, budgets need to be tied to the library's strategic plan and assessment goals, discussed in part 2 of this book. These are, in turn, tied to the strategic plan and goals of the larger organization. Any money allocated by the library should clearly help to achieve these larger aims.

## Approaches

The two most common budgeting approaches are incremental budgeting and zero-based budgeting. Each approach has strengths and weaknesses. Some directors vary their approach from year to year, and some use the same one again and again. In reality, most directors probably use some combination of these two—meaning they start from the prior year's budget, but require some degree of justification from middle managers related to both new and ongoing expenses.

## Incremental Budgeting

Incremental budgeting is an approach for creating a budget based on how much was spent in previous budget cycles. The budgeting process starts with the allocations and expenditures from the previous year. Cuts and additional allocations are made based on budget priorities for the new year, and only changes are reviewed. This is the type of budgeting most people use in their home budgets, and has the benefit of making budget forecasting easier.

The drawback of this approach is that a library may spend excessively on things that need further review. For example, a library could carry an annual allocation for binding for years, without reconsidering whether or not it actually should bind anything. Another drawback to this approach is the impact it may have on middle managers. When people get in the habit of receiving a certain amount of funding, year in and year out, they may start to think of it as "their" money. This causes problems when the time comes for cuts, because middle managers are losing "their" money. This approach also disincentives cost savings on the part of middle managers, because they lose money if they find cost efficiencies.

## Zero-Based Budgeting

In zero-based budgeting, the director starts from zero at the beginning of every fiscal year, and requires managers to put together a new, complete budget request annually, no matter how much they spent or were allocated in the prior year. The benefit of this type of budgeting is that middle managers are required to review and justify every allocation, every year. They are less likely to fall into the trap of thinking of this as "their" money, and it creates more incentive for managers to find cost efficiencies. This can be especially useful in years when there is a budget crunch, since it requires each area of the library to review every expenditure to determine its value.

The drawback with zero-based budgeting is that it can make budget planning a more difficult and time-consuming process. A new budget is created every year. This also makes it difficult for managers to predict what their budget will look like from year to year. This lack of certainty can be stressful and can impact their autonomy and their ability to plan over the long term. Just as library executives tend to thrive more with greater determination related to their libraries, middle managers often thrive with the same determination. Zero-based budgeting impacts that.

In addition, there are some other approaches to budgeting, separate from those described above. Formula budgeting, or budgeting based on statistical inputs, is not frequently used to create library budgets, but is often used by state governments when funding public universities. In these instances, the number and type of students enrolled at the university equal a certain amount of funding for the institution. When libraries do use this type of budgeting, it is often for budgets related to faculty requests, where the number of students and faculty in a department determines the amount allocated for faculty requests or collection budgets for that department.

Performance funding is another type of budgeting that is in vogue for state and local governments. This type of funding looks at outputs rather than inputs. In other words, the library's impact in increasing financial awareness or literacy in the local community might be tied to the funding it gets from a local government, or a university's graduation rate may increase the library's state allocation.

Program budgeting might be used by the institution, particularly in higher education. This type of budget is directly correlated to the mission and strategic goals of the institution. Funding is allocated based on these goals, and must be demonstrated to support and further these goals.

In practice, most library executives probably use some combination of all these types of budgeting. For instance, collection development allocations for books might be developed annually by an acquisitions librarian using a program-based approach, since book budgets are goal-oriented and those goals might change from year to year. Database budgets, on the other hand, probably use an incremental approach, since those expenses tend to rise somewhat predictably from year to year. Travel and training budgets are almost always zero-based, because different employees pursue different opportunities, and many libraries use an annual request process to determine how these funds are budgeted. To learn more about types of budgeting, expenditures, and approaches, Robert Dugan and Peter Hernon's *Financial Management in Academic Libraries* is detailed and thorough (2017).

## Benchmarking

Benchmarking a budget against what other, similar organizations are spending on the same category is one particularly important step in the budget planning process. This ensures that the library is following best practices in allocating resources. It also ensures that when, for instance, the CFO calls to say that the library is receiving 60 percent more money for salaries than it needs, because no other library spends that much, it's easy to show that the salaries are right in line with other, similar institutions. Even better if the salaries are a few percentage points below the median expenditure, so that the library can show it is actually saving some money.

The best way to benchmark a budget is to become familiar with the major data sources that report on budgeting trends for the type of library. For academic libraries, this is the ACRL's Academic Library Trends and Statistics Survey, which has a nice data tool that is available for a small annual fee, called ACRLMetrics (2020). For public libraries, this is the Public Library Data Service, available from PLAMetrics (2020). The most useful part of these tools is the ability to create groups of libraries that are peers, so that the data is tailored to the specific situation. For public libraries there are also state-level surveys that are useful for benchmarking in a particular region, such as Texas State Library and Archives Commission's Texas Local Public Library Statistics.

There are also benchmarking tools that allow directors to look at salary data, such as College and University Professional Association (CUPA) salary surveys, Association of Research Libraries (ARL) salary surveys, and ALA-APA salary surveys. These are a perennial necessity, particularly when employees are asking for a raise. They can help justify the raise, or identify where a raise is not warranted. For an excellent, in-depth discussion of data-driven budgeting, see *Financial Management in Academic Libraries* (Dugan and Hernon 2017).

## Plan Ahead

Forecasting future budgets is essential when making the current year's budget, particularly in a climate where library budgets do not increase on a regular basis, or may be consistently decreasing. This is because there are two basic types of spending: one-time expenditures, such as purchasing a book or a new computer, and continuing expenditures, such as subscriptions or staff salaries. One-time expenditures only impact this year's budget. When a single book is purchased, the library won't need to pay for it again next year, though it may spend money on books more generally every year. If that spending is cut in a subsequent year, the book doesn't go back to the publisher, though the library may not get any more books. Continuing expenditures, on the other hand, impact future budgets. If someone new is hired, that person expects to get paid every year. If a database subscription is added, it must be funded on a recurring basis. If the money gets cut, that position or database is lost.

For this reason, making draft budgets or a spending plan for one or two years past the current year is a good idea. This allows a director to explore what happens next year if a position is created, but the budget is flat. Can the library afford that position and still cover increases in database costs if there's no new money? What if there's a budget cut? Is the position so important that it's needed regardless? If so, which database is cut when the overall allocation shrinks? All of these questions are immensely important to the library's future financial health, and should be answered before new positions or databases are added, because continuing expenditures are hard to cut once created. A contraction in service is almost always worse than never expanding the service in the first place, because patrons get attached to services.

When creating future forecasting budgets, remember to include cost increases in every category where they are relevant. This includes databases, employee benefits, memberships, software, salaries, and many others categories of expenses. Another consideration is whether there are any major expenses in the next few years, such as new security gates, a new integrated library system, or a library renovation. Be sure to include emergency funds. There are not many things that are certain in the library, except this: one major, unexpected expense every year. For a more in-depth discussion of forecasting, read the chapter titled "Revenue Sources" in William Sannwald's *Financial Management for Libraries* (2018).

## Stakeholder Buy-In

The more middle managers, and even individual library employees, have input on the budget, and the more transparent the decision-making process related to the budget, the more buy-in from these stakeholders. This is easier in years when the budget is healthy, much more difficult in years where it's lean, but the lean years are when this transparency and buy-in become most important. Those are the years when the director needs to know that everyone is rowing in the same direction. People become scared and start to panic if they don't know what's going on. Honesty and allowing input go a long way.

Even entry-level library employees can and should be involved in the budgeting process. Allow all employees to make budget requests for programming, equipment, travel, and training. Designate an allocation for supplies for each employee. This allows them to choose pens and notepads that meet their preferences, and is an inexpensive way to provide some autonomy that makes people happier at work. An award might even be created for employees who come up with the best way to save money to incentivize budget efficiency.

For middle managers, a discretionary budget, even if it's quite small, can help promote feelings of self-determination. This can also motivate these managers to find ways of saving money, because they can apply savings to an area goal or priority that is unfunded or underfunded. Though not all budget processes within libraries need to be formal, they should all be transparent and participatory.

# ⊚ Reviewing and Tracking a Budget

The lucky director will have a dedicated administrative assistant, business coordinator, office manager, or accountant who tracks expenditures on a day-to-day basis, and sounds the alarm if the money is running out. If the director is that person, then he or she must come up with a way to track debits and credits in real time, just like the last page in a checkbook. QuickBooks is a well-known and easy-to-use software program for this purpose. A book keeping class at a local community college might also help those who are really struggling.

If administrative support is available to track these expenditures on a day-to-day basis, and if the employee in this position is trusted to competently manage accounts and report back any problems, monthly or quarterly budget review is probably sufficient. During these reviews, discuss how spending is going in each category. Decide if any allocations need to be increased or decreased. Factor in any unexpected expenses. Part-time employee wages, for instance, tend to need regular revision, since someone may be out sick for a week or two without pay, or a part-timer may need to work more than usual if a full-time employee goes on leave.

Sometimes, emergency funds are left over at the end of the year. With each budget review, consider what will be done with this money if it isn't spent, and know if it needs to be spent before the end of the fiscal year. Have an easily executable plan for spending it.

# ⊚ Accountability

Many libraries are affiliated with government entities, either at the local or state level, that should provide accountability requirements related to the handling of cash and the spending of money. Sometimes these requirements may seem like red tape or busywork, but it's actually incredibly important to take them seriously, and to make sure that employees take them seriously. Many organizations have rolling audits, meaning that a library's financial practices can be reviewed at any time. Staying as "audit ready" as possible is the best way to ensure that no negative findings come back later.

## Documentation

Most organizations require documentation whenever money is spent. This may include an invoice or quote; a requisition, credit card statement, or authorization for payment; and a receipt showing that the correct amount was paid. In other words, something showing the cost, that the purchase was authorized, and that the correct amount was paid. Similarly, most organizations require that documentation is held for a specified amount of time in case of an audit. Know these requirements, and follow them.

With all of this paperwork, it might be tempting to simply sign whatever gets put on the desk. This is a terrible habit. Review everything that is signed, and understand how to double-check the information provided. Remember that if something has the director's signature, and funds are misappropriated, the director is the liable and responsible party. Blindly signing can create a lot of problems.

Similarly, do not let employees spend money without reviewing their expenditures. Either the director or a middle manager needs to track all outgoing funds. Spending authorizations are key, as are processes to review credit card statements. If the director doesn't know what an expenditure is on a credit card statement or other document, this must be found out.

## Separation of Duties

One cash-handling concept every director should know is separation of duties. The more duties held by one person in relation to money, the easier it is for that person to misappropriate funds. Giving different oversight duties to different people is key to making sure that all of the library's financial resources are being received and spent appropriately. For instance, never let someone with a credit card approve his or her own credit card expenditures. A library director with a credit card must have a supervisor outside of the library review monthly credit card reports. This also means that someone who receives cash should not be responsible for preparing a deposit, and someone who prepares a deposit should not be responsible for reconciling accounts. In practice, libraries need to ensure that there is oversight at each stage of the process, and that duties related to cash and procurement are split among multiple employees.

Don't think of this as an exercise in distrust for employees, and don't present these measures in this way. This is really a way to keep employees safe from allegations of financial malfeasance. Oversight is as much to protect them as it is to protect the institution. Dugan and Hernon (2017) provide more information about managing a budget and budget accountability.

# ⑥ Key Points

- Budgeting doesn't have to be overly complicated. Library directors must determine the best way to do it based on their own strengths and competencies.
- Planning ahead and benchmarking can help ensure that a budget is strategic, forward-looking, and based on best practices.
- Accountability may seem like extra layers of red tape, but is incredibly important to ensure the integrity of the library and of individual employees.

# ⑥ References

Association of College and Research Libraries. 2020. "ACRLMetrics." https://www.acrlmetrics.com/.

Burger, Robert, Paula Kaufman, and Amy Atkinson. 2015. "Disturbingly Weak: The Current State of Financial Management Education in Library and Information Science Curricula." *Journal of Education for Library and Information Science* 56: 190–97. JSTOR.

Dugan, Robert E., and Peter Hernon. 2017. *Financial Management in Academic Libraries: Data-Driven Planning and Budgeting.* Chicago: Association of College and Research Libraries. ProQuest Ebook Central.

Hussey, Lisa K., and Diane L. Velasquez, eds. 2019. *Library Management 101: A Practical Guide.* Chicago: ALA Editions. Kindle.

Public Library Association. 2020. "PLAMetrics." https://www.plametrics.org/.

Sannwald, William. 2018. *Financial Management for Libraries.* Chicago: ALA Neal-Schuman. EBSCO eBook Collection.

# Getting Support

IN 2009, A SERIES CALLED SHARK TANK DEBUTED ON ABC. The premise is that entrepreneurs present business ideas to a group of investors, who decide if they're going to provide funding. Airing for twelve seasons as of this writing, the show's most compelling aspect is the drama of small business owners trying to persuade wealthy investors to believe in them and provide capital to further their business plans. The show made famous the idea of the five-minute pitch, or a brief summary of a business endeavor to garner support. Though this reality show might seem far removed from a small library somewhere in the middle of the country, in reality, the library director's job often feels just like this: constantly trying to "pitch" the library to people who hold the power to fund it, for better or worse. Selling the library means getting support, which equates to more money and more leverage. While most directors understand intrinsically the value of what the library offers, it can be difficult at times to translate that into words that each "shark" a director works with understands. Add to this the complexities of showing impact, and the whole proposition becomes time-consuming and trying.

When considering each library's "sharks," it's important to recognize both internal and external stakeholders. External stakeholders in particular, and especially those with some degree of power or influence, should be the responsibility of the director. These are the people that have the potential to make or break the efforts of the library. The leader of the library must be its best representative and advocate to the VIPs who control funding and access to other resources. In addition to these high-ranking officials and other VIPs, the director must take close responsibility for the relationship the library has with the community at large. The way the community feels about its library indirectly determines the level of funding the library receives, because the patrons are the customers. If they aren't buying what a library is metaphorically selling, then the library's efforts are already sunk. The library leader sets the tone and exemplifies the approach to developing meaningful, productive relationships that lead to buy-in and ultimately, better support.

## Definitions

Buy-in: Active support of a leader, leadership approach, or management decision.

Impact: The library's effect on its community.

Participatory leadership style: A democratic leadership style that allows for many people to have input regarding decisions and practices.

Return on investment (ROI): A business concept where the benefit of an investment is divided by the cost of the investment, resulting in a ratio or percentage that shows the value of an investment.

## Buy-in from Library Staff

Discussing the library staff first in this chapter might seem like an odd choice. Surely, the support of patrons, politicians, and other administrators determines funding more directly than the buy-in of the staff. The reality is that, though the director is often an externally facing position—and for good reason—overlooking the role of staff as stakeholders, and therefore people with whom the director needs to obtain support, is a huge oversight. In many ways, all of the other supportive relationships enjoyed by the library begin with the degree to which staff members support the goals and mission of the institution. If staff are dedicated and motivated by the vision of the director, then good relationships with the community, administration, and potential benefactors blossom. If not, none of these other relationships develop well, because they hinge on having excellent staff carrying out the director's plan.

Getting the support of staff may seem like the purview of new directors, or of directors who have lost trust for some reason. This is, however, a career-long endeavor. Staff turnover, changes in context, and different stages in the life of a library all impact the degree of support a director has at any given time. For this reason, directors should always seek to understand the level of backing they receive from staff, and to grow this base as much as they can.

To increase the degree of staff support, directors must first understand the view staff have of them, as well as their doubts. There are different ways of doing this, though probably one of the best is to gather anonymous feedback from the employees. This is most commonly done through an anonymous survey that focuses on the strengths and weaknesses of the leader. Though a director could create his or her own survey, using an established measure is helpful, especially one purpose-made to evaluate staff support for leadership. Established surveys provide baseline data that can help place the evaluation received in context, such as the IDEA Feedback System for Administrators (2021).

These surveys must be totally anonymous to gather honest feedback. This means that, though the leader receiving the data might be tempted to directly confront people who may have provided less-than-flattering input, this impulse must be resisted. Instead, the information gathered should be taken in a spirit of collegiality and growth. Problems and issues are to be addressed broadly, without trying to call out individuals who may have raised them. Responding to this feedback with professionalism and a degree of humility helps staff trust that their input matters and, in turn, develops staff support for the director and the wider goals of the library. As with any survey, it is always a good idea to make one or two visible, if small, changes right away based on the feedback, to show respondents that the information they provided is being considered and heard. Larger changes that take longer to implement may follow, of course, but this immediate response is a way to, again, show staff that the director is listening and that their input means something.

Another way to build the support of the staff is to involve them in decision-making. A participatory leadership style shows staff that what they feel matters, and that they are helping set the goals that they are expected to meet. If the goals are already set, or staff don't have the expertise to make a participatory leadership style work, a leader can also try to implement activities to help staff connect to the goals that have been set and take ownership of these. This might involve giving staff the autonomy to figure out how to achieve these goals on their own, in a way that makes best sense to them. This might also include providing training or mentorship for employees who might one day gain the expertise to take on further leadership roles. Whatever road this takes, staff must feel that they have ownership over their areas of authority to the highest degree possible in order to get the best buy-in for the larger goals of the library. Staff who feel devalued, overlooked, or unable to impact the activities of the organization are much less like to buy in.

Finally, many library leaders garner support by proving themselves as library experts, deserving of the related degree of respect. In other words, they show those who work for the library that the leader is a librarian's librarian—someone who understands the day-to-day struggles of librarians in the trenches, and can hold their own with their staff in this regard. Telegraphing a degree of solidarity with the staff is one way to gain respect and support for the overarching goals that have been set.

## ⑥ Upper Administration, Board Members, and Other Important People

In theory, the relationships directors have with upper administration, board members, and other people in positions of power should be easy. After all, the director's goals align with those of all of these other leaders. Of course, in reality, these types of relationships aren't easy at all. Horror stories abound about the poor situations that can arise, including budget cuts, impossible edicts, and general misunderstandings about what libraries actually do. This is especially problematic because these types of leaders often determine the library's funding as well as the opportunities the library has to grow. Suffice it to say, these relationships are vital, but often incredibly fraught.

So how does a library leader grow the relationships with these administrators in meaningful ways, resulting in a real understanding of the library and its value? Fundamentally, the cornerstone of the relationship a director has with the upper administration of the institution needs to be a clear understanding of what the library does for the patrons and, ultimately, for the administrator him- or herself. Of course, library leaders know how they support their communities. The administration also needs to know this.

The director's job is to make sure that whenever these types of people think of the library, they think of the value their students or constituents get from it. Not the cost, and not the problems, but the value only, or at least primarily.

The first step toward ensuring that administrators think of the library as a value proposition, and not simply a significant cost, is to make sure the library staff support the library, discussed in the previous section of this chapter. If staff buy in, they provide the best possible service for the community. If the community buys in to the value of the library, this is recognized by the administrators who are in charge of funding and other resources, especially if they are elected officials or if they are concerned with things like enrollment. A happy staff translates to a happy customer base, which translates to a more supportive administration, since the community is ultimately everyone's boss.

Along with this, the library's problems must be as self-contained as possible. Though it is always wise to let the administration know about potential issues, that doesn't mean that these should become the administration's concern. Library directors need to handle problems in-house and let the administration know about the solution, in case the solution doesn't work as well as planned. If the administration or board is involved with the library primarily through a set of unending problems, their view of it takes the shape of a problem. Getting advice is one thing, but library leaders who pass on their concerns to others do so at their own peril. This includes real crises, such as a massive budget cut. While honesty with administration about the potential impact of such a cut is important, if a cut comes down, the library director must figure out how to take it and move forward. Making the cuts someone else's problem by passing on the hard decisions about what is impacted to higher-up administrators won't get the library anywhere.

The most important thing for a director to remember is that the job of the library leader is to sell the library, as much as possible, to the people that make decisions. Figure out what impresses the leadership, and obtain a constant stream of the data, stories, or other information that makes the case. The last part of this chapter deals with demonstrating impact—take it to heart! Librarians are sometimes viewed as quiet people, but to ensure that the value of these institutions are understood, the good news must be quantified and broadcast from the rooftops.

Finally, directors can always make the job of administrators easier by being proactive in finding savings, opportunities for engagement, and other efficiencies. If an administrator views the library as an entity that works within the institution, and can help solve problems rather than creating them, the library is much likelier to garner support. Finding ways to create a new position without requesting new money, for example, can help an administrator who is probably already strapped for cash. If there's a budget cut coming, library directors can restructure their finances and provide a figure that they think they can reasonably remit. While this runs the risk of giving back more money than would have otherwise been cut, it also builds goodwill and might forestall further cuts down the line, if the administration is likely to listen to the director when he or she says the library can't take another cut. A library director who works with the administration, rather than trying to simply defend the library's territory from the administration, generally does a lot better, and gets buy-in in return.

Even with all of these actions, it's possible that a director will still experience a perilous relationship with administrators. There are some administrators who simply don't see the value in the library, no matter what the director does. In cases like this, community members, and especially benefactors such as big donors or local politicians, can be of particular value to ensure the library's interests are protected and supported.

Getting support for the library from the community is simultaneously the most difficult job of any library leader, and also the easiest and most natural objective in the world. By and large, people want to like the library, and people who use the library really love it. That said, getting these people to take their purported love of the library and turn it into meaningful, actionable support that helps the library achieve its goals when it comes to institutional support through funding and resources, is another story altogether. People love the library, and they will remind their presidents and mayors of this when the library is facing a catastrophic budget cut or the imminent shuttering of a facility. However important these rare, crisis-fueled moments are to a library's ongoing survival, the quieter, sustained support of patrons who regularly remind the administration that they would be up in arms at the first sign of such a crisis is the real golden ring for a director. Directors must always remember that how the community feels about the library on a day-to-day basis, during the good times and the bad, is pivotal to how much overall support the library receives.

The first important method to ensure the support of the community is to provide excellent customer service. If the members of the community know that the library works for them, they support the library. Conversely, a library that is dysfunctional pushes away community members and loses support quickly. Conducting regular surveys, focus groups, and other assessments of the sentiments of community members is extremely important to gauge how well the library is doing in this respect. Good leaders know the value of a multitude of assessments, and they take the feedback they get from these seriously. There is no point in doing such evaluations if what is reported isn't used to make decisions and improve. Other types of data can also be used to gauge whether users are coming in and using services. A drop in the number of circulations or computer use can indicate dissatisfaction or disaffection. Beyond assessments, leaders need to listen to patrons during everyday interactions. When users express that there is a problem with the library, believe them. Usually a repeated complaint from a few regular patrons is expressing the point of view of many other, quieter ones who might have simply stopped coming. Never discount a complaint, especially one received from more than one community member. In the same vein, if patrons say they really need or want a service, do whatever can be done to keep it. Again, a few comments can easily represent the point of view of many other people.

Another important factor in getting support from the community and keeping it is capturing the enthusiasm of the most loyal library users. This enthusiasm is generally expressed through a friends of the library group, but may also show up at community events, summer reading clubs, fundraisers or, again, in the day-to-day service operations of the library. Identifying these super-enthusiastic users and putting them to work as ambassadors and protectors of the library is so important to ensuring that the library has the backing of the larger organization. Again, these are the people that will likely make the largest fuss when the library's budget is threatened, and these are the people that help hold the fundraisers. They want outlets for their excitement—provide them with those outlets. Directors should also respect them for all they do, and cultivate their admiration on a personal level. If they believe in the vision and goals of the director, they are the best allies—outside of the library staff—to achieve these goals. Public libraries might find these types of people in a particularly active friends of the library group, while an academic library probably has them among the faculty. A really motivated group of faculty can be the best ambassadors to encourage library use and integrated library instruction.

They can also make quite a fuss when a budget cut threatens the subscription to their favorite journal or database.

Making sure the library is transparent and communicates its successes to the community at large is important, as with all of the other groups discussed here. Patrons might simply see the library as the place where they go to pick up the next best-seller, not an active, central hub of their community. Libraries with strong marketing plans make sure that the community knows who they are, what they do, and where they're going. Libraries that don't market well, even if they are successful in every other way, run the risk of keeping their worth hidden from the very people to whom it means the most.

One final note on ensuring community support. As mentioned above, every library has a small group of naturally enthusiastic patrons whose support is baked in. Every library also has the opportunity to create further groups of enthusiastic users who might become library ambassadors. The best way to do this is to keep community members engaged. Hold interesting programs, and do new and exciting things. Don't simply rest on what has been done in the past. Librarians who stay apprised of the professional literature, and look for opportunities to innovate, earn the respect of the users they engage, who might not have otherwise thought of the library as an organization worth that level of enthusiasm.

## ⓖ Support from Politicians and Benefactors

The final group discussed in this chapter could be described as the rich and powerful. They are often both. These people are potential "guardian angels" for a library, and libraries that have the support of one or more of these people are extremely lucky. This is especially true for small libraries that might not have a lot of authority or power otherwise. Many libraries inherited this kind of supporter, or the benefactor just showed up one day, eager to help. This doesn't mean that this kind of relationship can't be cultivated—only that many libraries, especially smaller libraries, are gifted these relationships, rather than pursuing them in an intentional way.

The first thing to remember when talking about benefactors is that there are others in a government organization or on a campus who help establish these kinds of relationships. Often, offices like a campus's alumni services may be aware of community members who have a particular interest in a library. They are also able to steer leaders away from people who may not be worth speaking to, or who already give to the organization in another capacity and who the library might need to stay away from. Remember, these relationships often involve monetary gifts, but not always. Cultivating the support of important community members without any expectation of a financial consideration often has its own, immeasurable value. They have influence in ways that can help a library, especially in a crisis that requires such a "guardian."

The second thing to remember is that benefactors and politicians are just people. Benefactors likely have one or a few charitable or community causes that they embrace, and the director needs to show how the library contributes to achieving the goals they have set for these causes. Politicians probably have one main goal, which is to remain in office or achieve higher office. In this case, the director needs to show how the library is so beloved that supporting it is bound to help them achieve reelection—again, this might be a good opportunity to use data that demonstrates impact. Smart people with money, influence, and power recognize and respond to good data. Note that the appropriate tone to take with such people is respectful and businesslike, rather than obsequious and flattering. Many people in such positions can spot toadyism from a thousand feet away.

The third thing to remember is that sometimes the cost of these relationships is higher than they are worth. Let's say a benefactor supports the library, but only if the library agrees to install a 30-foot-high piece of installation art they have created, which requires a custom-made display platform and new, elevated roof for the building. This benefactor's price might be too high. A good leader carefully weighs the costs and benefits of cultivating a relationship and identifies the ones that just aren't worth it.

## ⑥ Demonstrating Impact

One of the best ways to get support from the various constituents described above is to demonstrate impact. Just like on *Shark Tank*, libraries with a strong narrative about the difference they make are likely to get the most support. Unfortunately, though, demonstrating impact seems simple at first glance, but gets more complicated the more it is considered. To start with, what does impact really mean in the context of a library? How do libraries help students or the community? And how can librarians quantify the good work that we do? This section talks about the different ways the value of a library's services can be quantified, but ultimately, each library will have its own method to show its worth. Whatever way is chosen, remember that the better a library can demonstrate impact, the more resources that library is likely to get and the better support from the parent organization, whether that is a government, school district, or institution of higher education.

Demonstrating impact is different than what a library does when creating an annual institutional assessment plan or another assessment-based report, discussed in chapter 10. Whereas that type of assessment really looks at the weaknesses and strengths to direct management decisions across the library, the kinds of data used to demonstrate impact should focus more on the value provided for patrons. For public libraries, this might be a calculation that demonstrates the benefit to taxpayers. For universities, this is likely to be data that shows the library impacting student success, retention, or learning.

The library might be able to repurpose the data used for annual assessment activities to demonstrate impact, but might not present this data in the same way. It is most effectively demonstrated when shaped and curated. Context is vitally important. For instance, in the 2015 fiscal year, 37 million people used the New York Public Libraries. This is a huge number on its own, but it's much more impactful when one knows that only 9 million people attended major professional sports games that same year (Dwyer 2015). This shows how libraries can have a bigger impact on their communities than sports stadiums, which often receive far better funding.

This leads to the first concept related to impact: ROI, or return on investment. ROI is a business concept whereby the benefit of an investment is divided by the cost of the investment, resulting in a ratio or percentage that shows the value of an investment. Investments have a better ROI when their benefit far exceeds their cost. For libraries, ROI means demonstrating how the benefit that libraries provide to their communities is greater than the cost of maintaining and running them. To calculate ROI for libraries, first create an economic valuation that looks at the library's services and resources. There are several good resources to help guide a library in creating this valuation, including *Proving Your Library's Value* (United for Libraries, Fishel, and Wentworth 2020). There is also an online calculator from the ALA that can assist with this task (Massachusetts Library Association 2020). These valuations are very useful because compared to the cost the benefits of libraries to their communities are often significant. When one can show that the library serves a broad group of taxpayers, it helps to make the argument for the value of the institution.

For school and higher education librarians, discussions of impact often come back to student learning. How is the library contributing to what students learn? At academic libraries, student learning should be one of the central pieces of annual assessment, and the data collected through these activities can be repurposed to demonstrate impact. Again, context is important when presenting this data. For instance, a director might do a study of student citations from a hand-chosen group of classes that have or have not received information literacy instruction. This would look at the quality of citations in papers for students who received instruction, and in those for students who did not. For the purpose of demonstrating impact, the director would take this data and show how the library succeeded in improving citations for students. Maybe the director would even find out what grades the students earned to see if better citations are correlated to better scores. The way a director contextualizes and interprets the data is going to make a big difference.

Showing student success can be really tricky, although there are some good resources on the topic, including the reports from ACRL's Assessment in Action program, *Academic Library Contributions to Student Success* (2015), *Documented Library Contributions to Student Learning and Success* (2016), and *Academic Library Impact on Student Learning and Success* (2017). Showing other kinds of impact can also be difficult. Directors have to be careful to choose data actually showing a clear link—remember, correlation doesn't equal causation. For instance, just because seniors who frequently use the library live five more years than the average elderly person in the community doesn't mean that the library is the key to long life. It could be that seniors who attend the library are already in better health, which allows them to get out of the house more, and use the library more. Be thoughtful when constructing assessments.

Though demonstrating impact is often a big and complicated topic, not all data that shows impact has to be complex. Less intricate calculations, like how many library resources are used annually per potential library user or the percentage of the service population that uses the library each year, can help create a narrative for the library in the minds of the administration. These measures can also supplement the main-impact calculations the director performs, whether those are based on ROI or student success. Finding different ways to present data the library has already collected can be incredibly valuable.

Also remember that sometimes, showing impact requires thinking outside of the box. Sharing qualitative data along with quantitative data can help put a human face on programming. For instance, let's say the library runs a free tutoring program for elementary school students. The director can obtain qualitative feedback from the parents of those students, in addition to quantitative data about the program's impact. The words of the parents whose kids are served may be more effective than all of the numbers provided in terms of getting buy-in from upper administration.

## ⊚ Key Points

- One main job of the library director is to get support for the library from staff, administrators, community members, and benefactors.

- Buy-in from library staff is key to winning all other kinds of support, since staff carry out the director's vision.
- Administrators often support the library if they understand how the library supports them.
- Support from community members is important every day.
- Demonstrating the library's impact through data can be one important way to get support.

## References

Association of College and Research Libraries. 2015. *Academic Library Contributions to Student Success: Documented Practices from the Field.* Prepared by Karen Brown with contributions by Kara J. Malenfant. Chicago: Association of College and Research Libraries.

———. 2016. *Documented Library Contributions to Student Learning and Success: Building Evidence with Team-Based Assessment in Action Campus Projects.* Prepared by Karen Brown with contributions by Kara J. Malenfant. Chicago: Association of College and Research Libraries.

———. 2017. *Academic Library Impact on Student Learning and Success: Findings from Assessment in Action Team Projects.* Prepared by Karen Brown with contributions by Kara J. Malenfant. Chicago: Association of College and Research Libraries.

Dwyer, Jim. 2015. "Denying New York Libraries the Fuel They Need." *New York Times*, April 23. https://www.nytimes.com/2015/04/24/nyregion/denying-new-york-libraries-the-fuel-they -need.html?_r=1.

The IDEA Center. 2021. *Feedback System for Administrators.* Manhattan, KS: The IDEA Center.

Massachusetts Library Association. 2020. "Library Value Calculator." American Library Association. http://www.ala.org/advocacy/library-value-calculator.

United for Libraries, Alan Fishel, and Jillian Wentworth. 2020. *Proving Your Library's Value: Persuasive, Organized, and Memorable Messaging.* Chicago: ALA Editions.

# Peer Review, Accreditation, and Assessment

P RESUMABLY, TO BECOME A DIRECTOR IN A LIBRARY, one would already have a strong understanding of strategic planning, continuous improvement, and impact. This chapter focuses on peer review and accreditation, two assessment activities that often fall largely on the director, and probably aren't as well understood by new leaders. These tasks can be daunting, but they aren't as difficult as one might think. The key, as with many other areas, is to understand how to approach them for the best results. This chapter starts with peer review, and then turns more directly to accreditation.

Unlike some of the other chapters in this book, there is no popular movie or funny anecdote that discusses the sobering topic of peer review and especially accreditation. When considering further the possibility of an accreditation movie, one understands why. Such a movie would bore viewers to tears. That said, within administrative circles in higher education, the accreditation visit is viewed with a great deal of admiration and respect, though also with quite a lot of trepidation. This is because peer review is at the core of what educational institutions stand for: real evaluation of how well goals have been met, and where things can be done better. This is all to say that, despite the fact that it will never make a great movie, peer review as an assessment tool is vital to a successful library. This chapter only begins to touch on this topic. *Reviewing the Academic Library* by Eleanor Mitchell and Peggy Seiden (2015) is a much deeper dive.

## Definitions

Accreditation: An official recognition of an entity as meeting standards set out by an organization responsible for quality reviews in a domain.

Audit: A review of information about an organization to determine whether it complies with a set of standards or requirements.

Evaluators: Peer reviewers in quality and improvement processes.

Peer Review: Evaluation of something by outside reviewers who are experts in the domain.

Subject accreditation: Accreditation from a subject-specific entity.

Standards: Enumerated statements defining the criteria institutions must meet in order to gain and keep accreditation.

## The Role of Peer Review

All librarians are familiar with the concept of peer review. How many times a week does a typical librarian help patrons find that peer-reviewed journal article they need for a class or research project? Peer review, in the context of assessment, is essentially the same thing as peer review of journal articles, just on the institutional level. Going through a library peer review may be one of the best ways to evaluate it, because the director can get feedback from leaders at other, similar institutions about the operations and services offered.

The process of peer review takes many different forms, depending on why a library is doing it and what the focus is. Libraries are often involved in lots of different peer review processes. For instance, a library might go through an institutionally mandated peer review as a part of an assessment cycle or to maintain accreditation. During an audit of a city or county government, the library could get pulled into a peer review of financial practices, or maybe it is competing for a national grant that requires a periodic review by outsiders of a specific set of services, such as early-childhood programs. In all of these cases, other library professionals from outside the institution are brought in to help identify how well this set of goals is being accomplished. As these examples show, directors take part in many different kinds of peer review during the course of their career.

Because peer review can be such a valuable tool for leaders, ensuring that the library is periodically reviewed in this way is quite helpful. This peer review should be designed to bring in new ideas and help ensure that the library hasn't grown too insular, leading to decision-making that might be divorced from best practices in the field. For many libraries, this comes in the form of periodic appraisal for the purposes of accreditation, either through the state for public libraries or through the institution's accreditor for academic libraries.

While accreditation reviews certainly provide a good idea as to whether the library is meeting the benchmarked standards set by these evaluators, having a separate peer review process for the library, different from accreditation, also has a purpose. Ideally, this occurs between accreditation reviews, and helps ensure that the library is staying prepared for accreditation. While this may seem like a daunting system to set up, it directs the focus of a library's leadership and identifies problems a director might face in a low-stakes context of their own creation, rather than later on during an accreditation visit. This type of peer review can also ensure that the library continues to follow best practices by helping the director learn about different ways of doing things at similar institutions. This is always one of the most helpful aspects of an accreditation review, and a self-created peer review process, occurring once every five years, can keep the focus on continued growth.

Usually, this type of process consists of three stages:

1. Writing a self-assessment report.
2. Selecting evaluators, and providing them with the assessment report and directions for vetting the report.
3. Hosting a site visit for these evaluators to come to campus.

Some peer review processes might use different stages, but these are the main components in most. If directors create a peer review process for their own edification, obviously the stages the process follows and the focus of the review is up to them. Some libraries are mandated to go through periodic reviews by the institution, their accreditor, or by another organization to which they belong. In those cases, a director should follow the process created by the organization mandating the review.

## Self-Assessment Reports

The cornerstone of any peer review of a library is the self-assessment report, and the key to any good self-assessment report is the clarity and honesty with which the report is composed. A self-assessment report that paints everything in a positive light, obscuring or outright lying about the reality on the ground, is not much use to anyone. In order to get the most value from any peer review process, the report has to be honest, concise, and focused.

If creating a peer review process, start with a goal statement. Ultimately, what does the director want to achieve by getting this outside feedback? Once there is a goal statement, create an outline with areas to focus on in the report, as well as directions for the evaluator in assessing the report. For instance, if a library is undergoing a generalized peer review, a director should recognize that reviewers won't be able to look at absolutely everything the library does. Let's say the goal is to improve the services, support, and resources provided to a student population. In this case, the director should provide information about public services, collections, collection development processes, technical support, and facilities. The director might also give some basic information about technical services, business functions, and budgeting, but probably only as it informs this central goal. In contrast, if the director is asking another library leader to come in and look at the library's finances and cash-handling procedures in preparation for a potential audit, the focus would be on those aspects of library operations. Focusing the report so that the evaluator isn't overwhelmed by a flood of information is important.

One activity that might help focus how a director writes a report is creating directions for the evaluator before beginning to work on the report itself. Whenever engaging someone from outside of the institution to come in and evaluate the library, the director must provide detailed instructions that point reviewers toward the route the director wants them to take. These directions should provide focused questions and concerns, as well as directives related to the expectations and format for the forthcoming feedback. By creating the directions first, the report can be tailored to them. The director can also avoid over-writing by providing too much information. If a part of the document doesn't contribute to the successful completion of the evaluator's task, then it probably doesn't need to be there, and should be removed. Probably the most valuable reason to create the directions for the evaluator before writing the report is the list of questions for the evaluator to consider when completing a peer review. These questions should include: Does the institution adequately provide instruction for its patron population? How does the institution evaluate the sufficiency of its collections, and is this evaluation effective to improve collections? How does the library ensure it is fulfilling its mission? These types of pointed questions provide key topics on which the director can focus the narrative. This ensures feedback that really interests the director.

When writing a peer review report, whether it's an internally driven process or mandated, such as accreditation, the writer must be clear, concise, and organized. Writing this kind of report is a balancing act because the director needs to provide exactly as much information as the accreditor requires, without providing anything extraneous. In order to do this, the writer must be an excellent editor. Do not use flowery language or engage in obfuscation. The most meaningful feedback is going to be about places of weakness or confusion. If a director knows he or she is a flowery writer, then engaging an outside editor to help cut back on any florid prose could be valuable.

Also remember that these reports are not just the narrative itself—they should also contain a plethora of supporting documentation to help reviewers make sense of the data provided to them. When providing evidence, only offer the pieces that reviewers need from the documents, and highlight the relevant information. This way, they do not search through reams of data just to find the piece of information discussed. This, too, is an art rather than a science. Really think about what is required, and what is not, as documentation is prepared.

## Evaluators

Though this is listed as a separate "stage," a library will probably choose (or be assigned) peer reviewers concurrent with the creation of the report. Engage peer reviewers fairly early in the process, and give them plenty of time to review the documentation. The happier a reviewer is, the smoother the process goes and the better the response the library gets.

There may be rules related to peer reviewers if the library is required by the institution to go through this process. If not, directors may still want to set up some basic guidelines to govern who participates. For instance, they probably don't want anyone who has worked for them, since the goal is outside input. Accreditors routinely require evaluators from outside of the state. Someone from an institution similar to the one being reviewed is desirable. That list of peer and aspirational institutions, discussed in chapter 5 on assessment, is a good place to start when looking for evaluators. Directors should also decide how many evaluators they want to engage. If they try to get too many, the process could become needlessly complicated, but with too few, they might not get a critical mass of meaningful feedback. A reasonable number for this kind of project might be two to five evaluators, though larger libraries could require more.

When engaging evaluators, make sure to be clear about expectations throughout the process, such as providing the report within a specified timeframe, giving evaluators a set number of days to review the report, certain formats in which evaluators are expected to respond, and whether they are required to come to campus for a site visit. Though site visits are common during this process, sometimes a written report in response to the self-evaluation is sufficient, and is certainly easier than trying to bring someone to campus for a few days to evaluate the library. Still, a site visit where evaluators are brought to campus so they can clarify points that are unclear, and can interact with staff directly, can be incredibly edifying. Sometimes an institution is easier to understand when seen on the ground. Decide whether the library has the resources and time to set up such a visit. Obviously, if this option is chosen, the institution pays for travel, and might also need to provide a stipend for evaluators in consideration of the time they are spending to assist with the review process.

If a site visit is chosen, be sure to require as short a visit as possible, and schedule well, so that no one's time is wasted. Plan for transportation and meals for the reviewers, as well as accommodations near campus. A useful site visit should include plenty of opportunities to interact with staff as well as patrons, upper administration, and community members. Just like with the report, whatever is planned for a site visit should have a clear purpose, with directions related to how these visitors should respond with feedback. Will they have a sit-down meeting with library leadership to discuss their findings? Will the library expect a report from them? Is there a set of questions to explore? Provide this information to the evaluators up front.

## Consultants

Consultants are, in essence, another type of peer reviewer. The difference between a peer review process engaging librarians from other institutions and those engaging a consultant is that consultants are usually paid quite a bit of money to look at one particular problem. They are also often expected to provide recommendations about how to deal with the issue. For instance, a library can hire accreditation consultants who look at the report and convey where they think the library is going to have issues. The difference between these reviewers and, for instance, system or regional colleagues who might give feedback informally, is that consultants are paid (a lot of money) to know what they're doing, and to provide structured, often directive feedback, though a director can take this feedback or leave it. Strongly directive feedback is not likely from other types of peer reviewers, though suggestions about how to do things better are common. If the library is going through major restructuring, experiencing serious problems, or engaged in a process that is very fragile and requires a good deal of complex contextual knowledge, consultants can be valuable, but they are expensive.

When hiring a consultant, clearly specify objectives, and clarify how much time should be committed to the project and the end product the library expects. Again, clearly setting expectations, providing the right information, and structuring the project to ensure that everyone is on the same page is important when engaging a consultant. It is also important to get a consultant whose expertise is trusted, so that the library doesn't go through a lengthy, expensive process only to disregard the advice provided. Common types of consultants involved with libraries are management and marketing consultants, especially those engaged by the larger entity to help out the organization as a whole.

# Accreditation

The major peer review process for all types of libraries, and the one that most people are familiar with, is accreditation. All kinds of libraries get accredited and are required to maintain accreditation, including public libraries, academic libraries, and school libraries. While the imperative to be honest in peer review self-assessments is always important, with accreditation it is essential. If there is only one thing to take away from this chapter, please let it be this: everyone absolutely, positively, with no exceptions, must be honest in their accreditation reports. Anyone who has worked in the domain of accreditation, even tangentially, has heard stories of people who violated the honesty imperative. These stories do not end well, for the institution or the individual. Do not be that person.

This said, as long as the director has no problems being honest, accreditation is not the terrible, horrible, no-good, very bad thing it seems. Many people enjoy the accreditation process, and everything it entails, though this may seem crazy. They find it to be really satisfying to get evaluated based on what they're doing, and to ultimately know that the institution is meeting its obligations to the students, faculty, or community. Accreditation is included in a chapter about assessment because it is a giant continuous improvement process. The point is to make sure the library is meeting the standards it needs to meet, and that it can do better if it doesn't quite meet the mark. Accreditors are not trying to "catch" you; they come to a campus every five years to improve your library. The opportunity to get better is really a gift, if the director knows how to make the most of it. Although a leader might ultimately appreciate the process, however, it won't necessarily be fun.

One may wonder why the institution subjects itself to accreditation at all. Why partake in a two- or three-year process, at the end of which the organization might be embarrassed by the results? The answer is money and resources. For universities to receive federal aid, they must be accredited by an organization approved by the U.S. Department of Education. For public libraries, accreditation often allows membership in state resource-sharing groups and electronic consortiums. Obviously, these are both pretty good incentives. Additionally, for universities, accreditation attracts students, allows certification of students in certain professions, and helps maintain the quality of educational programs. Accreditation also allows for the standardization of certain common practices across higher education, such as awarding credit hours, which provides the basis for the transfer of credit and other functions across institutions.

By the way, was this described as a two- or three-year process? In reality, it is an ongoing process that should never really end. In the good old days, accreditation was something that a library started working on a few years before the next visit. This is no longer the case. Nowadays, a director should be keeping the library aligned with accreditation requirements, and assessing how well it meets said requirements, on an annual basis. This includes completing that assessment cycle every year, which is a requirement for most types of accreditation, as well as making sure that staffing levels, collections, and services remain sufficient. A continuous approach to accreditation may seem like a laborious way to run a library, but the director is actually just putting out a little effort every year to make sure the library is still doing the right things, instead of putting in a lot of effort over a few years to fix everything that has slipped since the last review.

Let's say someone is a new director who has never been through an accreditation review. If that person is lucky, the next visit is several years down the line, giving the director time to make sure the institution is where it needs to be. Whether the visit is next year, or five years from now, the first thing to do is find the accreditation standards that concern the library. Look at everything that could apply. If working at a school or institution of higher education, it's likely that there are sections of the standards that pertain to the library but aren't explicitly library related, in addition to those sections that are clearly aimed at the library. For instance, sections about finances or assessment often encompass a wide array of units, including the library. Review all of these sections and all of the supporting documents put out by the accreditor to help understand the standards. In addition to the official documents, look for presentations at accreditation-focused conferences and meetings. Also, talk to colleagues in libraries at other institutions that have gone through the process before, as well as people on campus who know about it. One of the best things about accreditation is that the community of people that work in the domain are very open to helping other people understand the standards.

Once the standards are understood, determine the best way to review them every year to ensure the library remains in compliance. Keep in mind that the more familiar a director is with the standards, the more the director naturally thinks of them when making any big changes or offering new services and programs. Ideally, this becomes a routine part of the thought process. If there isn't a set method for evaluating whether the library remains in compliance, create one. Again, spending time now to ensure the library remains in compliance is going to save potential heartache later on.

After gaining a thorough working knowledge of the standards, a director can also help the institution avoid making changes to the library that run afoul of them. This might be one of the most important jobs of a library director: keeping the institution within the guardrails. Let's say that a director has an upper administration that wants a library of the future—totally digital, a room full of computer terminals, and no public services staff. The director's job in this case would be to calmly explain to the administration that while the library can probably convert its collection to primarily or entirely digital, that conversion does not allow for chucking all of the reference and instruction librarians, since accreditation standards commonly require at least a minimum of instruction and reference services. Also, study spaces probably need to be a part of that plan, since these standards also routinely encompass facilities.

The director might also look at whether the library has a history program or a specialized language collection for a niche community, because those types of resources are awfully difficult to find in a digital format. Is the library going to be able to meet requirements for collections if these are gutted? Though most library directors won't face such an extreme scenario, there are times when every director has upper administrators or government officials who want to push for something that jeopardizes accreditation. The director has to be able to push back when this happens. Even if the battle is ultimately lost, at least the director provided a well-reasoned professional opinion, making executive leadership fully aware of the consequences before they happen.

What if a new director arrives at an institution that has an accreditation review coming up in the next three years? A director might even land somewhere, and within a month get handed a packet and asked to write an accreditation report. Find the silver lining: this is perhaps the best way to learn about the new library and evaluate where it currently stands. In this case, the director needs to find out about the standards as quickly as possible. That is always the first step, because a director can't write anything until he or she really know what is expected. During this phase, the director should read some sections from other institutions, if these are available, so that they know the common ways of responding. Don't simply copy another school's section, however. Remember that these documents are highly specialized to a particular institution. It's common to use someone else's section as a basis for one's own, but copying word for word—just replacing the institution's name—is never sufficient.

Next, the director needs to complete an audit of the library to see where it meets the standards, and where it is in trouble. Be really honest here! Imagine the most detail-oriented, particular reviewer the library could get, and view the institution through those eyes. While that review is not likely, this exercise gets a director ready for the worst. To do an audit, break down each standard that involves the library into subsections—make sure to pay attention to each part of the standard. Incorporate anything that explains the sections, such as guiding questions, rubrics, or suggested documentation. Look at whether the required information can be gathered, and whether it fulfills the expectations of the accreditors. Share the results with fellow librarians to see if they have any further concerns, questions, or information that might make sections look better than the initial audit suggests.

After the audit, focus on the weak areas. This includes areas where the library has a policy or procedure that is sufficient to fulfill the requirements, but it isn't written down. Remember the general rule for accreditation: if it isn't written, it doesn't exist. There may be true weak areas in the library. Divide those into two categories: those that can be remediated with relative ease, whether through further resources, a change in policy, or another alteration; and those that can't be remediated before a visit. Tell upper administration about both types of deficiencies, but the latter are much more serious—hopefully, the library won't have many of those, if any.

Obviously, if things can be fixed, fix them. If this isn't possible, find ways to mitigate the issue as much as possible. For instance, let's say the library skipped a few years in the formal assessment process. The director can't go back and do this assessment as though it was done at the time, but can do it retroactively if he or she is honest about when it was completed. The director can also look at other types of informal or formal assessment completed or participated in that year, such as a new strategic plan or assessment tied to grants. This is, frankly, not ideal—the reality is that the library may still experience issues with accreditation in this situation, but at least the institution is working toward a solution. Perhaps the best thing a library could do here is faithfully complete any future years of assessment to show that it has remedied the problem.

Once weak areas are identified and remediated, start writing the accreditation report. Everyone has a preferred method when writing these documents. One way is to outline the report based on the supporting documentation from the accreditor first, and then to pull headings for the sections from the key points called out in this documentation. This is helpful for two reasons: first, it ensures that key points are covered, and second, it makes it very easy for the evaluator to see that these relevant points are discussed. Another approach is writing a draft with everything that one might need, and then go back with a metaphorical paring knife and prune out anything that is not essential. Be really ruthless at this stage—sections might lose 25 percent to 50 percent of what has been written. After that, reorder sections and work on headings. Finally, double-check what has been composed against the supporting manuals from the accreditation group to make sure each piece of every required question is answered. These are just a few possible suggestions. Everyone must find the process that works best for them.

When approaching an accreditation section, one key element is the standard itself. For instance, the Southern Association of Colleges and Schools Commission on Colleges (SACSCOC) has the following standard for libraries: "the institution provides adequate and appropriate library and learning/information resources, services, and support for its mission" (2017, 26). Go through and highlight the important words in this standard that need to be addressed: adequate, appropriate, resources, services, support, and mission. In this case, the requirement is to show that the library has both adequate and appropriate resources to support the mission, as well as adequate and appropriate services and support. In addition, the standard calls for the writer to connect these resources, services, and support with the university mission. Each part of this prompt needs to be addressed. Writers can gain further insight by looking at the resource manual, which provides guidance.

Once the section is written, gather documentation and prepare it. Though every accreditation organization has its own guidelines related to supporting documentation, in general, only provide that which is necessary to prove the argument. Also highlight the part of the document that is relevant, and only include the pages from the document that contain evidence. This helps to focus the attention of readers directly on what they need to see, and keeps them from looking at other, irrelevant sections.

After the document is submitted, a library might have evaluators come to campus. As with the peer review visit, approach these visitors as colleagues who have a sincere interest in making sure the library's operations are of high quality and meet the standards set out by the accreditor. They are not there to "getcha." They want to have a dialogue, learn how the library does things, and provide an opportunity to improve if necessary.

## ⑥ Other Peer Review Processes

There are lots of different peer review processes that the library might be a part of, in addition to those mentioned here. The library may be involved in subject accreditations for academic departments, city peer review processes, peer review associated with program review in higher education, or certification visits. Though the above two sections focus on specific instances of peer review, the included suggestions should apply to all kinds of review. They are all similar, though the focus might change. Remember, the key principle with any peer review is honesty—nothing wonderful can come from peer review without honesty.

## ⑥ Key Points

- As with academic journal articles, peer review is the gold standard for library assessment and evaluation.
- Self-assessment reports should be clear, concise, and honest.
- Accreditation compliance and review should be a continuous process.
- When preparing for an accreditation review, first audit the library's compliance with the standards. Next, fix any problems that can be fixed. Then start to write.
- Make sure documentation is clear, and only provide the page or pages required to provide evidence.

## ⑥ References

Mitchell, Eleanor, and Peggy Seiden. 2015. *Reviewing the Academic Library: A Guide to Self-Study and External Review*. Chicago: American Library Association.

Southern Association of Colleges and Schools Commission on Colleges. 2017. *The Principles of Accreditation: Foundations for Quality Enhancement*. Atlanta: SACSCOC. https://sacscoc.org/app/uploads/2019/08/2018PrinciplesOfAcreditation.pdf.

# CHAPTER 19

# Developing Professionally through Upper Management

THOUGH THE LEVEL OF DIRECTOR OFTEN SEEMS LIKE the highest aspiration for librarians, many reach this level and realize that they want to advance even further in their careers. This, of course, takes a librarian out of the library, which can be difficult for someone whose identity is tied up in being a librarian. Still, one of the best ways to advance the cause of libraries is to send more people to the ranks of city manager, provost, or principal. After all, an executive leader who comes from the library understands the needs of the library in a way many others won't, and can advocate with a more powerful voice. Though the road to advancement is not always clear, there are some things that librarians can do to help their case once they have reached the director level.

This chapter presents different modulations of the same theme which is that advancement is predicated on being viewed as more than just a librarian. This is not to say that being a librarian is a negative thing. Many, if not most, of the skills that librarians are known for lend themselves to advancement into leadership positions in the organizations that contain libraries. However, many librarians view themselves as only librarians, and fail to branch outside of this comfort zone in a way that prepares them to succeed in other roles. To advance, a director must find ways to branch out.

This means, develop skills outside of the library. When opportunities present themselves to take on authority that is larger than or more central to the overarching organization, take them. As with every other level of management, leaders at this stage are cultivated through such projects. Furthermore, directors often don't have the full breadth of knowledge required to lead the larger organization. This knowledge must be gained. For instance, in higher education, the dean of a library needs to learn about enrollment management, faculty issues, curriculum development, accreditation, and a host of other topics to advance—these are all requisite for a provost. Library leaders who don't branch out and develop outside of the library don't gain these competencies, and never make it into executive leadership. Similarly, a public library director without deep knowledge of city funding, and not just funding for the library, is not likely to advance to city manager.

Library leaders who want to advance must also understand the organization as a whole. Though librarians in executive management are important to the ongoing advocacy of libraries, they can't simply manage as librarians. Sometimes, the library budget needs to be cut in order to fund another department or project. As a director, a librarian should recognize that what is good for the library is not always good for the organization.

Finally, librarians who wish to advance must telegraph their leadership ability, potential, and aspirations. People often assume that librarians want to stay librarians. Because it's a niche field, with practitioners viewed as dedicated to the profession, it is often assumed that librarians don't want to advance out of the library. Make clear that this is not the case. This means presenting oneself as a potential executive leader. Often, people give opportunities to competent, trusted colleagues who have communicated that they want those opportunities.

Though there are many things library directors need to learn to transition into a higher-level role, directors also have plenty of experiences compared to other administrators that can be quite beneficial for a provost or city manager. For instance, library directors are often responsible for extremely complicated budgets that require in-depth understanding of financial rules across the institution. They are also proficient with licensing and contracts in ways that faculty and other administrators are not. Most importantly, the positive aspects of libraries, and especially the service orientation that is so essential to the profession, can make one a better leader at all levels. The good does not need to be let go to advance. Often, librarians make excellent leaders in other areas of organizations because of their ability to find, arrange, and communicate data, as well as their dedication to serving others with collegiality. Ben Franklin, among many other fine librarians across history, exemplifies the type of leader a strong librarian can become.

# Bibliography

Abbajay, Mary. 2018. *Managing Up: How to Move Up, Win at Work, and Succeed with Any Type of Boss*. Hoboken, NJ: Wiley. EBSCO eBook Collection.

Allan, Barbara. 2017. *The No-Nonsense Guide to Project Management*. London: Facet Publishing.

American Library Association. 2020. "Disaster Preparedness and Recovery." http://www.ala.org /advocacy/disaster-preparedness.

Association of American Colleges and Universities. 2009. "Information Literacy VALUE Rubric." https://www.aacu.org/value/rubrics/information-literacy.

Association of College and Research Libraries. 2015. *Academic Library Contributions to Student Success: Documented Practices from the Field*. Prepared by Karen Brown with contributions by Kara J. Malenfant. Chicago: Association of College and Research Libraries.

———. 2016. *Documented Library Contributions to Student Learning and Success: Building Evidence with Team-Based Assessment in Action Campus Projects*. Prepared by Karen Brown with contributions by Kara J. Malenfant. Chicago: Association of College and Research Libraries.

———. 2016. "Framework for Information Literacy for Higher Education." January 11. http:// www.ala.org/acrl/standards/ilframework.

———. 2017. *Academic Library Impact on Student Learning and Success: Findings from Assessment in Action Team Projects*. Prepared by Karen Brown with contributions by Kara J. Malenfant. Chicago: Association of College and Research Libraries.

———. 2020. "ACRL 2019–20 Academic Library Trends and Statistics Survey." https://acrl .countingopinions.com/.

———. 2020. "ACRLMetrics." https://www.acrlmetrics.com/.

Association of Research Libraries. n.d. "About LibQual+." Accessed November 21, 2020. https:// www.libqual.org/about/about_lq.

Bertalanffy, Ludwig. 2015. *General System Theory: Foundations, Development, Applications*. Revised Edition, New York: George Braziller Inc. Kindle.

Blair, William M. 1957. "President Draws Planning Moral: Recalls Army Days to Show Value of Preparedness in Time of Crisis." *New York Times*, November 15. ProQuest Historical New York Times.

Bonner, Michael. 2020. "Paul McCartney Says He Still Consults John Lennon When Writing Songs." *Uncut*, November 12. https://www.uncut.co.uk/features/paul-mccartney-still-con sults-john-lennon-128539/.

Brooks Jr., Frederick. 1995. *The Mythical Man-Month: Essays on Software Engineering*, Anniversary edition. Boston: Addison-Wesley.

Brustein, Darrah. 2018. "How Warren Buffett and Steven Spielberg Used Strategic Relationships to Launch Their Careers." *Forbes*, January 10. https://www.forbes.com/sites/darrah

brustein/2018/06/10/how-warren-buffett-and-steven-spielberg-used-strategic-relation
ships-to-launch-their-careers/?sh=2cf169cb267a.

Burger, Robert, Paula Kaufman, and Amy Atkinson. 2015. "Disturbingly Weak: The Current State of Financial Management Education in Library and Information Science Curricula." *Journal of Education for Library and Information Science* 56: 190–97. JSTOR.

Burton, David H. 1995. *Clara Barton: In the Service of Humanity*. Westport, CT: Praeger. EBSCO eBook Collection.

Butin, Dan. 2016. "So You Want to be a Dean?" *Chronicle of Higher Education*, January 13. https://www.chronicle.com/article/so-you-want-to-be-a-dean-234900/.

Cameron, Kim S., and Robert E. Quinn. 2011. *Diagnosing and Changing Organizational Culture: Based on the Competing Values Framework*, 3rd edition. San Francisco, CA: Jossey-Bassey. Kindle.

Conger, Kate. 2018. "Google Removes 'Don't Be Evil' Clause from Its Code of Conduct." *Gizmodo*, May 18. https://gizmodo.com/google-removes-nearly-all-mentions-of-dont-be-evil-from-1826153393.

Creswell, John W., and J. David Creswell. 2018. *Research Design: Qualitative, Quantitative, and Mixed Methods Approaches*, 5th edition. Los Angeles: Sage Publications.

Cummings, Marissa. 2020. "A Look Back at Hurricane Harvey's Impact in the Coastal Bend." *KIIITV*, August 25. https://www.kiiitv.com/article/news/a-look-back-at-hurricane-harveys-impact-in-the-coastal-bend/503-79556696-0870-4747-b6cb-29861d99bbcb.

Deutsch, Morton. 2009. *The Resolution of Conflict: Constructive and Destructive Processes*. Carl Hovland Memorial Lectures Series. New Haven, CT: Yale University Press.

Dobson, Michael Singer, and Deborah Singer Dobson. 2000. *Managing Up!: 59 Ways to Build a Career-Advancing Relationship with Your Boss*. New York: AMACOM. EBSCO eBook Collection.

Dugan, Robert E., and Peter Hernon. 2017. *Financial Management in Academic Libraries: Data-Driven Planning and Budgeting*. Chicago: Association of College and Research Libraries. ProQuest Ebook Central.

Dwyer, Jim. 2015. "Denying New York Libraries the Fuel They Need." *New York Times*, April 23. https://www.nytimes.com/2015/04/24/nyregion/denying-new-york-libraries-the-fuel-they-need.html?_r=1.

Federal Emergency Management Agency. n.d. "FEMA Media Library." Accessed November 20, 2020. https://www.fema.gov/multimedia-library.

Fey, Tina. 2011. *Bossypants*. New York: Little, Brown and Company.

Finklestein, Sydney. 2016. *Superbosses: How Exceptional Leaders Master the Flow of Talent*. New York: Portfolio/Penguin.

Franklin, Benjamin. 1732. *Poor Richard's Almanack*. Reprint, Mount Vernon, NY: Peter Pauper Press, 1984.

Gallo, Carmine. 2017. "Steven Spielberg's First Boss Made This Promise That Unleashed the Director's Creativity." *Forbes*, October 9. https://www.forbes.com/sites/carminegallo/2017/10/09/steven-spielbergs-first-boss-made-this-promise-that-unleashed-the-directors-creativity/?sh=1d89f65a46d7.

Gilbert, Erik. 2019. "Assessment Is an Enormous Waste of Time." *Chronicle of Higher Education*, March 20. https://www.chronicle.com/article/assessment-is-an-enormous-waste-of-time/#:~:text=The%20fundamental%20claim%20of%20the,courses%2C%20curricula%2C%20and%20colleges.

Goleman, Daniel, Richard Boyatzis, and Annie McKee. 2013. *Primal Leadership*. Boston: Harvard Business School Press. Kindle.

Halford, Macy. 2010. "'Reading became Fashionable': Ben Franklin and the Privatization of Libraries." *The New Yorker*, September 27. https://www.newyorker.com/books/page-turner/reading-became-fashionable-ben-franklin-and-the-privatization-of-libraries.

Hernon, Peter, Ronald R. Powell, and Arthur P. Young. 2004. "Academic Library Directors: What Do They Do?" *College & Research Libraries* 65: 538–63. EBSCO Education Source.

Hill, Linda A., and Kent Lineback. 2019. *Being the Boss, with a New Preface: The 3 Imperatives for Becoming a Great Leader.* Boston: Harvard Business Review Press.

Hussey, Lisa K., and Diane L. Velasquez, eds. 2019. *Library Management 101: A Practical Guide.* Chicago: ALA Editions. Kindle.

Karsh, Ellen, and Arlen Sue Fox. 2019. *The Only Grant-Writing Book You'll Ever Need*, 5th edition. New York: Basic Books.

Kuh, George. 1995. "The Other Curriculum: Out-of-Class Experiences Associated with Student Learning and Personal Development." *Journal of Higher Education* 66 (2): 123–55. JSTOR.

———. 2008. *High Impact Educational Practices.* Washington DC: Association of American Colleges & Universities.

Kwak, Young Hoon, John Walewski, Dana Sleeper, and Hessam Sadatsafavi. 2014. "What Can We Learn from the Hoover Dam Project That Influenced Modern Project Management?" *International Journal of Project Management* 32: 256–64. ScienceDirect.

Lavariega Monforti, Jessica L., and Javier A. Kypuros. 2019. "10 Suggestions for a New Academic Dean." *Chronicle of Higher Education*, August 25. https://www.chronicle.com/article/10-suggestions-for-a-new-academic-dean/.

Lencioni, Patrick. 2002. *The Five Dysfunctions of a Team: A Leadership Fable.* San Francisco, CA: Jossey-Bass.

Lewin, Kurt. 1947. "Frontiers in Group Dynamics: Concept, Method and Reality in Social Science; Social Equilibria and Social Change." *Human Relations* 1 (1): 5–41. SAGE.

Lewin, Kurt, Ronald Lippitt, and Ralph K. White. 1939. "Patterns of Aggressive Behavior in Experimentally Created 'Social Climates.'" *Journal of Social Psychology* 10: 271–99. Taylor & Francis Online.

Lewis, Andy, and Maya Anderman. 2016. "Discovered by Spielberg: How a Lucky Encounter with the Director Launched These 6 Stars." *Hollywood Reporter*, May 6. https://www.hollywoodreporter.com/news/discovered-by-spielberg-a-lucky-891580.

Massachusetts Library Association. 2020. "Library Value Calculator." *American Library Association.* http://www.ala.org/advocacy/library-value-calculator.

Mintzberg, Henry. 1978. "Patterns in Strategy Formation." *Management Science* 24 (9): 934–48. JSTOR.

Mitchell, Eleanor, and Peggy Seiden. 2015. *Reviewing the Academic Library: A Guide to Self-Study and External Review. Chicago*: American Library Association.

National Center for Education Statistics. 2020. "IPEDS Data Collection System." https://surveys.nces.ed.gov/IPEDS/.

OCLC. 2018. "Assessment Tools." https://help.oclc.org/Librarian_Toolbox/OCLC_Usage_Statistics/140Assessment_Tools?sl=en.

*The Office.* 2006. "Booze Cruise." Netflix video. 21:02, January 5. https://www.netflix.com/title/70136120.

Parker, James F. 2008. *Do the Right Thing: How Dedicated Employees Create Loyal Customers and Large Profits.* Upper Saddle River, NJ: Prentice Hall. Kindle.

Public Library Association. 2020. "PLAMetrics." https://www.plametrics.org/.

Quinn, Robert E., and John Rohrbaugh. 1981. "The Competing Values Approach to Organizational Culture." *Public Productivity Review* 5 (2): 122–40. JSTOR.

Reale, Michelle. 2013. *Mentoring and Managing Students in the Academic Library.* Chicago: ALA Editions. Kindle.

Rider, Fremont. 1944. *The Scholar and the Future of the Research Library: A Problem and Its Solution.* New York: Hadham Press.

Salkind, Neil J., and Bruce B. Frey. 2019. *Statistics for People Who (Think They) Hate Statistics*, 7th edition. Los Angeles: Sage Publications.

Sandberg, Sheryl. 2013. *Lean In: Women, Work, and the Will to Lead.* New York: Alfred K. Knopf. Kindle.

Sannwald, William. 2018. *Financial Management for Libraries.* Chicago: ALA Neal-Schuman. EBSCO eBook Collection.

Schein, Edgar H., and Peter A. Schein. 2016. *Organizational Culture and Leadership.* Hoboken, NJ: Wiley. EBSCO eBook Collection.

Schneid, Frederick. 2005. *Napoleon's Conquest of Europe: The War of the Third Coalition.* Westport, CT: Praeger.

Searcy, Carly Wiggins. 2018. *Project Management in Libraries: On Time, On Budget, On Target.* Chicago: ALA Editions.

Sider, Laura. 2020. "How Many Books Are at Yale University Library?" *Ask Yale Library*, April 7. https://ask.library.yale.edu/faq/175105#:~:text=Our%20collection%20at%20Yale%20University,printed%20books%20to%20electronic%20databases.

Southern Association of Colleges and Schools Commission on Colleges. 2017. *The Principles of Accreditation: Foundations for Quality Enhancement.* Atlanta: SACSCOC. https://sacscoc.org/app/uploads/2019/08/2018PrinciplesOfAcreditation.pdf.

The IDEA Center. 2021. *Feedback System for Administrators.* Manhattan, KS: The IDEA Center.

Thomas, Kenneth W. 1988. "The Conflict-Handling Modes: Toward a More Precise Theory." *Management Communication Theory* 1 (3): 430–36.

Tucker-Jones, Anthony. 2019. *D-Day 1944: The Making of Victory.* Gloucestershire, UK: The History Press. EBSCO eBook Collection.

Tuckman, Bruce. 1965. "Developmental Sequence in Small Groups." *Psychological Bulletin* 63 (2): 384–99.

Tuckman, Bruce, and Mary Ann Jensen. 1977. "Stages of Small-Group Development Revisited." *Group Organization and Management* 2 (4): 419–27.

United for Libraries, Alan Fishel, and Jillian Wentworth. 2020. *Proving Your Library's Value: Persuasive, Organized, and Memorable Messaging.* Chicago: ALA Editions.

Zamoyski, Adam. 2005. *1812: Napoleon's Fatal March on Moscow.* London: Harper Perennial. Kindle.

# Index

# About the Author

**Bridgit McCafferty** is the dean of the University Library at Texas A&M University–Central Texas, and has led the library for eight years. Prior to this, she was in charge of reference and instruction services. She has taken on major administrative projects for her university, including recently chairing the Southern Association of Colleges and Schools Commission on Colleges (SACSCOC) Accreditation Reaffirmation Compliance Committee. She coauthored *British Postmodernism: Strategies and Sources*, and has written several book chapters about library assessment and library support for nontraditional students.